BEYOND BRILLIANCE:

THE BLUEPRINT FOR LEARNING ANYTHING

LUCAS MILLER

ILLUSTRATIONS BY LAUREN OUYE

Disclaimer

Contents

To my mother, who always encouraged me to be curious.

Introduction

In school, we are taught *what to learn*. Vocabulary, the Pythagorean theorem, Roman history, the periodic table. The list goes on and on.

But not once are we taught *how to learn*. How to pick up concepts quickly. How to effectively study. How to not waste our time.

I wrote this book out of anger, because I've been a student for over fifteen years now, and I never knew there was such a disconnect between "what science knows" and "what students do"—that there was a better, faster, and easier way to succeed in school.

Most people have a fixed mindset. They think everyone is born with a certain amount of intelligence and that's it. You're either smart or you aren't.

Scientists now know that this view is nonsense. Even if you think you're not intelligent, your brain has immense potential and an inherent ability to grow and strengthen itself; it just didn't come with an operating manual. You'll find such a guide to learning to your fullest potential in *Beyond Brilliance*.

This book is not *"20 Easy Ways to Become a Straight-A Student in No Time"*. It is also not a dense, unapproachable textbook that drones on and on about experiment after experiment before getting to the point. It is a science book—no doubt—yet it's organized into a collection of short essays that are illustrated and easy to understand. You won't find academic jargon or any mention of "experiential learning models" inside. Just practical advice you can use.

The tools and ideas in this book are for destroying the illusion that we cannot become smarter and that we cannot use our brains better and more efficiently. When we stop buying into this illusion, we *can* then become "learning machines"—people who approach learning systematically and work to continually expand their base of knowledge and challenge their worldview.

My goal is to bridge the gap between academic volumes (which contain useful scientific knowledge but aren't very user-friendly) and the many vague, worthless self help books on this topic. Consequently, the book is short and punchy; I want to introduce a new way of looking at the world without getting bogged down in excessive findings and examples.

If you're pressed for time, or aren't really that interested in the underlying science, you can go through this book in a weekend and put the *Beyond Brilliance* methods to use immediately. If you're like me and want to dive more deeply into the technical details, there are links to supplemental materials in the Notes and Resources chapters.

While the science of learning is still far from complete, thousands of researchers have agreed on certain principles. Yes, reliable techniques that you can use right now to get ahead of the others! If you are truly committed, this book can give you a new attitude about yourself, help you retrain your brain, and even change your life.

What you'll learn:
- What strategies you should throw out immediately
- Intelligence isn't fixed—it's something we can all develop over time.
- The best predictor of academic success (Hint: It's not effort)
- The *most practical*, *most efficient*, and *most inexpensive* ways to absorb material

- Why testing yourself is crucial
- How multitasking actually wastes time
- Surprising truths behind problem solving and creativity
- How snoozing more means studying less
- The key to rapidly learning foreign languages
- A host of productivity and technology tips, tricks, and hacks

You should view this book as a cookbook for learning, full of recipes for success. But everyone knows the best chefs don't follow instructions exactly. If a technique or suggestion doesn't quite fit your needs or circumstances, that's okay. In fact, you should expect to find information that you either don't like or doesn't work for you. Follow this book's lead and, when stuck, experiment. Adopt what's useful, reject what isn't, and add what is uniquely your own.

I wrote this book for one reason: to help you *learn how to learn*, which is a gift that will last you a lifetime.

This book will be particularly useful to you if you fit one or more of the following descriptions:
- You are convinced or have been told at some point in your life that you are not smart
- Math makes you cringe
- You frequently find yourself saying "I'm not an English person" or "I'll never be good at science"
- All you are trying to do is maintain a 3.0 GPA
- You think the only way to excel in school is to cram and consistently pull all-nighters
- You envy the people who manage school, sleep, a social life, and seemingly everything else with ease
- School comes easy to you and you are looking for techniques and strategies to supercharge your learning, test-taking, and productivity
- You are a graduate student who constantly needs to stay on top of new material
- You simply like learning and want to get better at it

In short, if you are a student of *any* kind, this book is for you.

It's time to rethink learning. Let's get started.

— *Lucas Miller, Cognitive Science and Entrepreneurship, University of California, Berkeley*

CHAPTER
FIRST

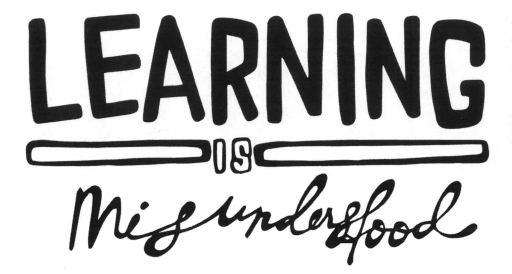

Much of what we consider gospel is horribly wrong

Most students approach learning in the wrong ways. Preferred methods, such as highlighting, underlining and rereading, turn out to be largely wasted effort. Even medical students, who spend an inordinate amount of time studying, tend to rely on techniques that don't serve them well.

Like most of my peers, I left high school believing that to study meant to pore over my notes and assignments as many times as possible. It seemed intuitive; if you expose yourself to something enough times, you can burn it into memory.

Mere exposure, however, does not guarantee the formation of memories. New research shows that this brute-force method of passive review is actually one of the most time-consuming and ineffective ones out there, as it gives rise to something called the *illusion of mastery*, where an individual mistakes a growing familiarity with the material for actual understanding.

In reality, the best learning techniques are not obvious, like waiting until you get a little rusty to review material or interleaving two different but related topics into one study session, but we'll get to all of that later.

For now, it's essential to know that your study strategy is based on beliefs about how you learn best. Whether or not you are consciously aware, you ask yourself and answer questions like: is going to class really worth it? do I benefit from reading the textbook? how much studying do I need before I've mastered the material?

The more accurate your beliefs, the more effectively you will learn (and make better grades and stay competitive in life). The more flawed your beliefs, the less effective your study habits (and the worse your grades and so on). Your beliefs can make you fail, or succeed.

You don't need to be naturally smart to succeed in school. You don't need to put in long nights and give up your social life to get top grades. You don't need to have a knack for a subject in order to do well in it. You can compete without sacrificing sleep. You can enjoy school, learn a lot, and lead a balanced life. I've proven it, and I wrote this book to show you how to prove it too.

Throw these out immediately

Regardless of whether you finish this book or not, at least read this section. And stop doing these things.

Introducing the villains:
1. Speed reading
2. Rereading
3. Highlighting
4. Underlining
5. Passive note-taking
6. Cramming
7. Brain games

Speed Reading

Kim Peek, the inspiration for Dustin Hoffman's character in the movie *Rain Man*, is the only confirmed speed reader in history. He was a savant who could read multiple pages at once and had near-perfect recall.

Now, I understand the allure of being able to breeze through whole books in one sitting. Who wouldn't want to be able to absorb information that quickly?

Unfortunately, like everything that seems too good to be true, the effectiveness of speed reading is a lie. What? All those popular websites and online courses that promise you can read upwards of one thousand words per minute with near-perfect comprehension are scams? Yes.

According to eye-movement expert Keith Raynor, the real limit seems to be around five hundred words per minute. After that, your eye muscles can't keep up. Your brain's limited mental RAM can't hold on to all of the material. Comprehension plummets[1].

If your goal is to learn, speed reading is useless. Just like with any other skill, the best way to become a better reader is to read. No other way around it.

Rereading

This is another insidious technique, although it has a far more powerful and legitimate grip on the public's mind.

The thinking behind rereading is simple: if you read a text enough times, you'll be able to cement it in your memory.

While there is evidence that rereading a piece more than once *may* aid comprehension, it's a terribly inefficient route to take. It is expensive time- and energy-wise and leads to the illusion of mastery. You should avoid this strategy whenever possible—we'll get to efficient ways of reading later.

I will say this though: I understand that some people like to reread books for pleasure, and that's perfectly fine. Rereading a fictional book is like watching a favorite movie for the second time. But if your goal is to learn and retain information without wasting time and energy, rereading is an awful choice.

Highlighting

Even though a textbook full of colored streaks looks like progress, highlighting is a dreadful time killer.

Look, I get it. Your first thought: "If it's marked, I'll be sure to remember that little nugget of knowledge!" Incorrect. The simple act of highlighting just isn't enough to move information into long-term memory. You're way better off making flashcards. It'll take a little longer, but you'll actually learn.

Underlining

Same as highlighting.

Passive Note-taking

Take extensive notes. Write down every little thing the teacher says. Don't reformat. Don't illustrate. Don't make any attempt to simplify. Don't do anything to the information presented (otherwise you might lose a critical piece of knowledge). This is how almost every student is encouraged to take notes. But this approach is wrong.

Why? Well, complexity makes learning *more* difficult, not less. Think for a moment: what happens when you try to remember what you just took notes on? Can you recall most of what you wrote—the main ideas—or do you feel you have to pull out the notes and look at them? I'm guessing the latter.

Don't get me wrong, writing things down is a great way to retain information. And there are ways of taking notes that are incredibly worthwhile. But if you're filling up notebooks with pages and pages of information and then never looking at them again, you're really doing yourself a disservice. Finding what you need when you need it is also going to be near impossible.

Cramming

We've all done it. Whether it's because of procrastination, laziness, unavoidable circumstances, or just a naive belief that it works, cramming is something we're all guilty of (at least once). The reasoning behind cramming is as follows: if you jam everything into your memory right before you need it, you'll remember it more easily.

Tragically, that's just not how memory works. Your brain needs time to process new information and make sense of it, and multiple review sessions are required to effectively transfer something into your long-term memory.

Cramming is like overpacking a cheap suitcase—you pack it full for a flight but it bursts upon arrival.

It's also like waiting until the night before a marathon to start training, or cooking a three-course meal with only milk, carrots, and beans, or trying to host the Olympics with only a few weeks of preparation.

But it's perhaps most like making a house by just stacking bricks on top of one another and then hoping it will survive a hurricane. Sure, it might survive a Category 1 or a Category 2 storm, but it's bound to topple at some point. The same goes for studying—cramming will give you a quick boost for the imminent exam, but you'll lose nearly all of the information shortly after.

Effective studying relies on two things: brief study sessions where neural "bricks" are laid, and time in between for the mental mortar to dry. *Binging and purging have no place in the successful student's toolbox.*

Another issue with cramming is that it almost always goes hand in hand with sleep deprivation. Getting enough zzz's is critical to learning and memory. All-nighters wreak havoc on your body and brain. Don't sabotage yourself. You are better off going to sleep and waking up early for a short, targeted review.

Brain Games

Brain training websites like *Lumosity* don't work. Sure, you might end up getting really good at rapidly clicking on a spot or categorizing items a certain way, but you won't become smarter.

What brain games do is make you good at those specific games, and that's all.

If you like playing games as a way to have fun and relax, then please, go for it. However, you shouldn't fool yourself into thinking that improving your crossword or sudoku skill translates into anything meaningful. Doing so only creates an illusion of competence, and any perceived gains in intelligence are almost certainly delusional.

Your thoughts

Before we dive into the material, take a few minutes to write down thoughts on learning.
- What does it mean to you?
- When is it easy for you? Difficult?
- Outside of school, what do you enjoy learning most? Why?
- Why do you think some people are better learners than others?
- How do you think you can stack the deck in your favor when it comes to learning?
- Who has the taught you the most in life? Do you have any mentors?

Keep your answers in mind as you read. We will answer these questions.

CHAPTER
MYTHS

Intelligence is fixed

In study after study, Stanford psychology professor Carol Dweck has shown that people subscribe to one of two mindsets:
1. Fixed mindset - the idea that you are born with a certain amount of intelligence and you really can't do much to change it.
2. Growth mindset - the notion that your intelligence is plastic and can be developed over time.

In the words of Dweck:

> In a fixed mindset students believe their basic abilities, their intelligence, their talents, are just fixed traits. They have a certain amount and that's that, and then their goal becomes to look smart all the time and never look dumb. In a growth mindset, students understand that their talents and abilities can be developed through effort, good teaching and persistence. They don't necessarily think everyone's the same or anyone can be Einstein, but they believe everyone can get smarter if they work at it.

In a series of experiments (detailed in her book *Mindset*), Dweck split students into two groups and tested them. Some kids were praised for their *intelligence*. "You must be smart at this", they were told after doing well on the test. The others were praised for *effort*. "Good job! You must have tried really hard."

All the students were then given a follow-up test that was much harder, designed for students two grades above. The "intelligence group" floundered. They gave up quickly, thinking "I'm not clever enough to solve this, I might as well just give up." They assumed their failure was evidence of not actually being smart. On the other hand, the "effort group" performed well. Not only did they get higher scores but they also tended to spend more time working on each problem. "I just need to try harder and then I'll get it", they told themselves.

After repeated trials with students of every class, race, IQ, and so on, Dweck found that praising intelligence over effort had the same negative impact on performance; even preschoolers weren't immune.

When kids are told they are "smart", they are celebrated for their innate "talent". They begin to define themselves by that description, and when times are tough or that image is threatened, they have trouble coping. Having to put out effort is public proof that they can't cut it on their natural gifts. So if an answer doesn't come to them immediately, they conclude "I must be dumb" or "I'm no good at this." Kids who have a fixed mindset are mainly concerned with how smart they are. They prefer tasks they can already do well and avoid situations where they might make mistakes or look uninformed.

Curiously, when students are praised for their hard work, and not only their hard work, but also their strategies, their ideas, their focus, their perseverance and commitment to the learning process, then they learn the ingredients of success. People who have a growth theory of intelligence want to challenge themselves to increase their abilities, and are fully aware of, and even comfortable with, the idea that they may fail at first.

The harm in having a fixed mindset:

> *I'm struggling. My grades are poor, and I continue to fail at everything I do. It all means I can't cut it. I'm just not meant to excel in school. Why even bother studying? I'm going to try less.*

The downward spiral continues.

The benefits of having a growth mindset:

> *Okay, I got a bad grade. I'm struggling. How informative! I clearly have more learning to do and maybe a different strategy will work better. If I try a little harder, then I'll get it.*

Progress accumulates over time.

Luckily, mindsets can be taught. A great example is Harlem in New York City. Harlem is a big, big town. Low incomes. High crime. Little hope. Hardly the place you'd go to discover a thriving education system. "For generations, our society has said to communities like this one, 'here are some teachers (but not enough) and here is some money (but not enough) and here are our expectations (very low)...good now do your best...'" notes entrepreneur and 18-time best-selling author Seth Godin. Few are surprised when this plan doesn't work.

But *Harlem Village Academies (HVA)*, a network of charter schools founded in the area, has succeeded. In founder Deborah Kenny's proud words, students at *HVA* start "several years behind grade level, but in just a few years are transformed, ranking among the highest in the nation—with 99% of eighth graders meeting proficiency standards in math, science, and social science." Kids who could barely read, had trouble paying attention, shared old textbooks, and didn't value school—completely changed—because they were taught a growth mindset.

Regardless of IQ, socioeconomic background, country of origin, shoe size, whatever, *all students (and not just those in school) can learn at high levels*—if they believe in and push themselves.

And now here's a surprise for you. By reading this section itself, you've just undergone the first half of a growth-mindset intervention. Simply knowing that the brain grows most by failing and making mistakes (and not by getting everything right) can begin to change a person's mindset. The second half of the intervention is for you to actually implement the change.

Now go, struggle and fail. Your brain will grow.

Brainpower comes in one flavor

How intelligent are you? Your answer probably depends on some kind of test score, something that labeled you early on as either gifted or average (or perhaps not that sharp).

Fortunately, the question is inherently not so simple.

In 1989, Harvard psychologist Howard Gardner described nine types of intelligence[1]:
1. Word smart
2. Number smart
3. Picture smart
4. Sound smart
5. Body smart
6. People smart
7. Self smart
8. Nature smart
9. Life smart

What other scientists thought were just soft skills, such as interpersonal abilities, Gardner realized were actually legitimate types of intelligence. It makes sense—just as a math whiz might be able to understand the world of physics, someone who is "people smart" is likely to understand and thrive in the worlds of sales and entertainment.

If you're interested, here are more detailed descriptions of Gardner's types of intelligence:

Linguistic ("word smart"): These people like to argue, persuade, entertain and instruct. They can find the right words to express what they mean. Think writers, politicians, and comedians.

Logical-mathematical ("number smart"): those who are good at reasoning, calculating, thinking in terms of cause and effect, creating hypotheses, and finding patterns. They are drawn to arithmetic, strategy games, and experiments. They like to be prove things and be right. Think mathematicians, scientists, and detectives.

Spatial ("picture smart"): People who can think in 3D such as artists, pilots, architects, and sailors.

Musical ("sound smart"): These individuals have a knack for discerning sounds, pitch, tone, rhythm, and timbre.

Bodily-kinesthetic ("body smart"): People who can control their bodies and handle objects carefully (e.g. athletes, dancers, surgeons, and craftspeople).

Interpersonal ("people smart"): Those who can understand and work well with others. They can sense people's feelings and motives and are often compassionate and socially responsible (or, on the flip side, manipulative and cunning). Think teachers, actors, and salespeople.

Intrapersonal ("self smart"): Those who can understand their own thoughts, feelings, and desires. Psychologists, spiritual leaders, and others in touch with themselves use this knowledge to set and achieve personal goals.

Natural ("nature smart"): Those who can recognize different kinds of plants and animals, make important distinctions in the wild, and use this knowledge productively. Think farmers, hunters, chefs, and Navy Seals.

Existential ("life smart"): Those who like to tackle the deep questions: what is the meaning of life? why are we here? what happens when we die? Philosophers, poets and priests fall into this category.

Each of these intelligences is unique and important. Unfortunately, IQ tests[2] and schools generally only focus on mathematical and linguistic intelligence. They praise the algebra whizzes and the Scrabble players and relegate those who don't fit the mold to "regular" classes and subpar teachers.

It's a fact that many truly brilliant people think they're not, because they've been put into a box and judged according to a particular view of the mind. Good news is, we know intelligence isn't about how many facts you can memorize or how well you can do on a standardized test— this is a dangerous belief that limits the potential of so many students. Instead it's about how you think and how well you can deal with new situations and learn from your mistakes, an ability that is hard to pinpoint and differs from person to person.

If you're curious about what kinds of smart you are, take a look at this checklist[3]. You may realize you have more intelligences than you previously thought or than people have told you.

If you can't win with the cards you have, move to a different table. It's never too late to rediscover your talents. You are not stupid. No one is.

Being good at a subject is a matter of inborn talent

"I've never been good at math", "Science isn't my thing", "She's an English girl", "He's got the language-learning gene". We hear these things all the time.

Many students think that they need an innate "knack" for a subject in order to do well in it. They believe that if they're not naturally talented in a field such as writing or math, nothing can be done to change that. They believe that if the material doesn't make sense to them immediately, they're screwed and should focus their efforts elsewhere. These notions couldn't be further from the truth.

Let's take the *2 Sigma problem* as an example. In 1984, the educational psychologist Benjamin Bloom found that students who received one-on-one tutoring performed on average more than two standard deviations better than the average student taught using traditional classroom methods. That's a fancy statistical way of saying that the average tutored student was above 98% of the students in the regular class[4].

Bloom tested students in different grades, at different schools, and with different cognitive abilities and attitudes toward school. Same exact result. Success in the classroom isn't about ability, it's about methods.

The real reason learning seems like an innate ability is because people figure out what comes easy to them early on and then stick with it. Conversely, people who start off bad at math learn to avoid it whenever possible, people who hated English class never pick up a book again, and people who weren't athletic as a kid learn to hate sports.

Whether you believe it or not, learning is a skill that can be cultivated. It is not simply an activity of the preordained few "geniuses". Being smart is a choice we can all make.

You need to learn according to your learning style

Take a moment to contemplate what kind of learner you are. Do you prefer a hands-on approach, or do you need to hear something aloud before it sticks? Do you turn immediately to books to learn about a new subject, or do you lean on pictures and graphs? Perhaps you don't fit any of these profiles, and you rely on other methods.

Belief in this idea that everyone has a preferred learning style is pervasive. It's recommended at all levels of education, and teachers are urged to offer material in as many different forms as possible to cater to the many different ways a student may learn best.

Well, I hate to be that guy, but the concept of different learning styles is one of the greatest neuroscience myths out there—up there with the notion that you only use 10% of your brain (you use all of your brain[5]).

In 2008, UCSD psychology professor Harold Pashler reviewed over fifty experiments on the learning style concept "from kindergarten to graduate school". Not one of them contained legitimate scientific evidence that you learn better if you receive information in a form that matches your preferred style[6]. The theory should be abandoned.

What does this mean? It means you can't use statements like 'But I'm a visual learner!" or "I took a test and learned that I was a poor auditory learner, so there's no point in me listening to a lecturer for more than a few minutes" as crutches anymore. Not only are they harmful, but they perpetuate a misguided sense of diminished potential[7].

Everyone is different, that is obvious. However, we all have large baskets of prior knowledge, interests, motivational levels, and other beliefs that shape how we learn and overcome setbacks. And while it's true that most of us have clear preferences for how we like to study, there are universal learning principles, supported by empirical evidence, that we can all use with great success, for free, today.

Left vs. right brain

It's the basis of all kinds of personality tests, self-help books and team-building exercises. Which one are you?

Logical, methodical and analytical—you're probably left-brained. You should go into science or accounting. Creative and artistic—right brain badge no doubt. How about pursuing a career in music or creative writing?

It's a deeply compelling model.

Trouble is, like most neatly-packaged explanations of complex concepts, it simply isn't true—a recent University of Utah analysis of more than one thousand brains undeniably confirms this point[8]. Regardless of personality or skill set, you use both the right and left hemispheres of your brain to perform everyday functions.

Just like learning styles, the misconception that everything to do with being logical is housed on the left, and everything to do with being creative is confined to the right, is a harmful one. When you self-identify as a "left-brainer" or a "right-brainer", all you're essentially doing is providing an easy, widely-believed excuse for why you can't do something. This excuse is especially tempting to use when learning a logic-heavy subject like math. "I'll never be good at this, I'm *way* too right-brained." Nonsense. There is hope. Art is all stick figures to you? You have a shot. Terrified of public speaking? As long as you practice, it *will* get easier.

Learning is supposed to be easy

It's not, even for "brilliant" people. Our brains are actually designed to learn best when we're operating at the edge of our abilities, stretched outside of our comfort zones, and when we're making tons of mistakes.

Just like writing a stellar term paper, starting a successful business, getting drafted into the NBA, finding your soulmate, or anything else good and desirable in this world, learning takes time and sweat. It's a *process*, where progress is incremental and setbacks are guaranteed.

Knowledge is just a bunch of isolated facts

Elon Musk, the founder of Tesla and "the modern-day Thomas Edison", compares knowledge to a tree. His response (to a Reddit question about why he is so smart)[9]: "I think most people can learn a lot more than they think they can. They sell themselves short without trying... Make sure you understand the fundamental principles, ie the trunk and big branches, before you get into the leaves/details or there is nothing for them to hang on to." Long story short: superficial memorization cuts it, until it doesn't, until you're forced to do more than bubble in the answer on a multiple-choice test, until true comprehension is tested.

Students often write out definitions on note cards (or make Quizlet sets) and memorize information as stand-alone facts. The problem with this strategy is that many teachers test for understanding, how concepts connect and build off of one another, cause and effect, and significance.

You really can't expect to be successful if you're just memorizing and regurgitating information—students who only do this will fail in school and life. If facts aren't connected by branches and supported by a strong trunk, you can't use them. Period.

John T. Reed, author of *Succeeding*, offers a crucial additional insight:

> When you first start to study a field, it seems like you have to memorize a zillion things. You don't. What you need is to identify the core principles – generally three to twelve of them – that govern the field. The million things you thought you had to memorize are simply various combinations of the core principles.

For example, all of economics is built upon six main tenets:

1. We live in a world with scarce resources.

> Land, water, fossil fuels, and other natural resources on Earth are limited.

2. There ain't no such thing as a free lunch.

> To get one thing that you want, you usually have to give up another thing that you want. You can't get "something for nothing". Even if something appears free, there is always a cost to you, to another person, or to society, even if hidden. Trade-offs are everywhere.

3. All choices have something called opportunity cost (what someone gives up by not going with the next best option).

> The cost of going to college isn't just the tuition, books, and fees, but also the forgone wages. The cost of seeing a movie is not just the price of the ticket, but also the value of the time you spend in the theater.

4. People respond to incentives in predictable ways.

> If stock prices fall, people will buy more. If they rise, people will buy less.

5. Market forces and economic systems influence people's decisions.

> If there is high demand for a particular job (and that job pays well), people will be more

likely to enter that field. In a strict economy like North Korea, where almost everything is owned and controlled by the government, most people don't have the choice to invest in the stock market.

6. People gain when they trade voluntarily.

This is why both buyers and sellers often say "Thank you!" after a purchase.

Once you internalize these core concepts, you can move on to more advanced ones: what price to choose for your product, how banks work, why a company might want to go public, etc.

The most beautiful, complex concepts in the universe are really just a bunch of basic ideas put together. You can learn much more than you think.

When you're learning, you'll know

Learning doesn't have to be purposeful. We learn all the time and often do so without any awareness.

Simple example: you suddenly get a new haircut. Nothing drastic, but different than your normal one. People notice. They compliment you (hopefully). How come? Because they learned what you look like; your face, your dress, your walk. And every time they see you, they compare what they see to what they *expect* to see. This time, there was an incongruity. It might have taken them awhile, but they noticed.

This kind of expectation violation happens all the time. As humans, we are constantly making predictions about our world, based on our volumes of knowledge and experience. When one minor thing is off, we think "Hmm, something's new..." and then we investigate.

Students like to think they know when they are learning and when they are not. A great deal of learning, however, occurs subconsciously. Think of a time when you struggled and struggled and then, finally, the "eureka" moment came. Everything seemed to click. You felt accomplished, like you really made it to the next level. What's interesting is that the real learning happened before the breakthrough—when you thought you weren't learning at all.

It's often the case that when you feel you're learning the least (when you're frustrated and uncertain and the material feels impossible to master), you're actually learning the most. We'll get to how to measure learning later. But for now, be happy knowing that *even if you don't think you're making progress, in reality you are*. All those hours struggling aren't for nothing.

Learning is like opening up your head and having stuff dumped in

In everyday use, learning has become synonymous with "taking in information". Knowledge is relayed from an authority (the teacher) to a learner (the student), generally by lecture. This thinking and practice are firmly entrenched in most classrooms, where students sit passively, listen, follow directions, and please the teacher by avoiding mistakes.

Taking in information, however, is only distantly related to learning. It would be nonsensical to say "I just read a book on swimming, now I've learned that" or "We went over the parts of Canada's federal government today, now I could run the country".

Real learning is something you do, not something that is done to you. It is constructive, not receptive, and involves a complex process of rediscovering material for yourself, connecting it to what you already know, and adding your own unique twist that makes it relevant *to you.*

Rote memorization is the best way to learn

Rote memorization is like trying to meet your daily calorie count by eating spinach. It's incredibly time-consuming and (although theoretically feasible) should not be your go-to strategy.

If learning by stuffing your brain with facts is the most effective way you know, or the only way you know, let me fix that right now. Here are a ton of additional (and superior) ways to learn that are more fun and take advantage of your various intelligences:

- Talk, read, or write about it
- Draw, sketch, or visualize it
- Dance it, build a model of it or do another hands-on activity
- Sing it, find music that illustrates it, listen to music while learning
- Relate it to a personal feeling or inner experience
- Conceptualize, quantify or think critically about it
- Work on it with one or more other people

"I am my course load"

You are not your IQ. You are not your SAT score. You are not a number.

You are not the school you go to, the school you just got admitted to, or the one you graduated from. You are not the courses you are taking. Your major is not your destiny.

You are not "pre-med", you're a person. A living, breathing, autonomous person. Who can grow and change and learn and lead.

Poor grades don't mean you are incompetent—you just have more to learn. Majoring in art or English doesn't mean you will fail in life. And choosing to study something you love over something practical won't prevent you from getting your dream job—you don't need to study X to become X (unless it is legally required).

Never confuse your track or your unit load or your GPA with your identity. You are much more than a mere snapshot in time.

Effort is the single most important predictor of academic success

"Try harder" is something we hear all the time. Got passed up for a promotion, "try harder". Failed to meet your weight loss goal for the month, "try harder". Not getting the grades you want, "try harder". After a while, though, we run out of energy for *harder*. No matter how hard we push and push, we come up short.

When it comes to learning, you can try as hard as you want, but if you aren't learning in learnable ways, you'll always come up short. Intention to learn is helpful, but not enough. Knowing how your brain actually works is fundamental.

Your school cares about you

Child labor wasn't eliminated in America for moral reasons. It was always cheaper to pay children. It made economic sense (sure, a few parents got incensed about eight-year-olds losing fingers and being abused on the job, but most business owners fought hard to keep kids at work).

Eventually working-class adults got angry though. These low-wage children were taking their jobs; this is precisely why compulsory public education was introduced in 1918.

Part of the rationale: let's educate kids now so they will become more compliant and productive workers when they grow up. We'll train them to be obedient, to memorize and to embrace the status quo. That way, when they eventually enter the workforce, we'll make more money and have fewer problems.

Don't believe me? Think about school for a second. The straight rows. Being grouped together by birthday. The bell system. Detention. It's a head start in getting used to authority before you enter the actual factory.

What you're taught in school:
- Use #2 pencils
- Don't forget to write your name
- Have neat handwriting
- Take notes
- Show up
- Get gold stars
- Don't get demerits
- Do as you're told
- Don't ask questions, especially "stupid ones"
- Don't say anything that might embarrass you or your friends
- Don't break the rules
- Don't challenge authority
- Cram for tests
- Don't miss deadlines
- Do the minimum amount necessary so you can get to the next subject
- Once you learn a topic, move on
- Participate in a large number of extracurriculars
- Get good grades
- Get into college
- Have a good resume
- Get a good internship
- Get a good job
- Pay your bills and taxes

The last generation this system worked for was our parents, but it's not 1945 anymore! The economy has changed. It needs problem-solvers, not obedient factory workers. Dreamers and builders and leaders, not office drones.

What you should do in school:
- Sign up for the classes you enjoy
- Ask questions
- Participate

- Stay after class
- Seek out interesting problems
- Pursue a hobby
- Teach your peers
- Listen to your interests
- Make something
- Work on a project
- Read in your spare time
- Doodle
- Dream
- Be brave
- Be curious
- Be you

Mass education was not developed to propel students to success or to create scholars. It was invented to churn out adults who were competent and could be told what to do and for how long, who worked well within the industrialized system and didn't ask questions.

As sad as it is, your administrators are there to pump you in and pump you out smoothly and safely. That's it. There are simply too many kids to do anything else—to push for better.

If you follow the rules and avoid making a scene, you will slip through the cracks.
If you don't take charge of your own education, you'll become a factory worker of tomorrow. If you don't make school what you need it to be *for you*, you won't have the life you dreamed of, or even a life you want.

CHAPTER
NEUROPLASTICITY

YOUR MIND — IS — PLASTIC

The brain you were given is not the brain you're stuck with

Barbara Arrowsmith Young was told in first grade that she would never be able to learn. Despite having a near perfect memory (she could reproduce the six o'clock news word-for-word at 11 p.m.), she couldn't "understand" anything, not even the relationship between the hands of a clock to tell the time. So on exams, she often got a 100%. Other times, whenever the test involved reasoning, logic, comprehension, or interpretation, she would get 10%. Her puzzled teachers gave her the strap for not trying. In high school and university, she disguised her disabilities by studying twenty hours a day.

At age twenty-six, the breakthrough came. After reading Aleksandr Luria's *The Man With a Shattered World*, a story about a Russian soldier who was shot in the head and developed severe disabilities, Young discovered that a part of her brain (responsible for analyzing incoming information and making sense of it) wasn't working properly. Then she read about the work of Mark Rosenzweig. In the 1950s and 1960s, the Berkeley researcher found that lab rats given a "stimulating" environment, with toys, ladders, tunnels, running wheels—the whole shabang—developed larger brains and performed better at learning activities than their friends in boring, normal cages. He concluded that the brain continues reshaping itself based on life experiences, rather than being fixed at birth: a concept known as neuroplasticity.

With the help of her mother and a teacher, Young devised brain stimulation exercises for herself that would work the parts of her brain that weren't functioning. She started with flash cards of two-handed clocks. She tested herself eight to ten hours a day. Gradually, she got faster and more accurate. Then, she added a third hand, to make the task more difficult. Then a fourth, for tenths of a second, and a fifth, for days of the week.

After three to four months, she noticed a fundamental change in her brain. She watched an episode of *60 Minutes*—and got it. Information became understandable. Reading got easier. She devised more exercises and found they worked too. Now sixty-five, Young has a masters degree in social psychology, has published a best-selling book, and has helped more than four thousand children with ADHD, dyslexia, dysgraphia, and other learning disabilities—kids dismissed as impossible to teach—overcome their diagnoses. Young is living proof that you *can* change the learner.

Mainstream science used to be sure brain structure was fixed. You had a set number of brain cells (called neurons) at birth; if any failed to develop, were injured, or died, they could not be replaced. Different brain functions were also localized to different physical areas of the brain. All things vision, for example, take place at the back of the brain, in a region called the occipital lobe. Emotion, speech, and language have their own distinct camps as well.

We now know that through experience, your mind continually reprograms itself[1], often for the better. With this knowledge, we've been able to:
- Raise IQs and circumvent learning disorders[2]
- Restore "sight" to the blind and "hearing" to the deaf (using a different sense to replace the one that doesn't work)
- Help the elderly sharpen their memories
- Restore paraplegics' ability to walk
- Cure cases of epilepsy

As we can see, transformations are not exceptions to the rule; they are the rule. The brain is not hardwired, it is livewired. It is born remarkably unfinished (unlike many animals who come pre-programmed and able to survive at birth) and can change, regenerate, grow, and remain "plastic"—even as you age. If a region "fails" or isn't being used, another one can come in and swipe it up, augmenting its abilities (this is why the blind tend to have keener hearing).

Every time you learn something, you grow new neural connections and strengthen existing ones. In fact, under the right conditions, learning a new skill can change hundreds of millions and possibly billions of connections between the neurons in our skull.

All of your experiences in life—from single conversations to your country's entire culture—shape the microscopic details of your brain. Every time you repeat a thought, or practice a movement, or acknowledge a feeling, you activate certain neural pathways. If those pathways get activated often, they reconfigure and strengthen, dominating other less travelled paths. They change your brain (for better or for worse). At the neural level, "who you are depends on where you've been" says David Eagleman, Stanford professor and writer of PBS's TV series *The Brain*.

You don't need drugs or an operation to change your brain (throughout life it remains a relentless shape-shifter), just a willingness to learn and reinforce good habits. We can all learn to become someone new, someone better, someone well adapted to the world around us. It's just a matter of whether we're willing to try.

Skills are built, not born

Skills, we've been told they are:
- Genetic
- Natural gifts
- In your blood/talents you are born with

Decades of science say that's all a load of crap. Riding a bike, dancing, shooting a bow and arrow, dribbling a basketball, public speaking—these are all *learned* skills.

And they are nothing more than connections and circuits in your brain. The more you fire those circuits, the better you get.

See, there's this awesome stuff called myelin, a fatty substance that wraps around the circuits you use the most, acting like an insulator that allows these cells to fire faster, better, and more accurately. As you improve at a skill, you develop more myelin around the relevant neuronal connections.

To be great at something is to be well myelinated. That's it. Instead of being pre-wired to be talented at certain things, which might be a horrible evolutionary gamble—imagine being born a talented writer in a society that only farms—our brains are designed to get good at what we do the most.

Sure, there are some natural advantages—height, body type, access to the best coaches, but as far as specific skills go, there are no gifts. Skilled people have more myelin, because they've practiced more and made more mistakes.

In *Outliers*, popular psychology writer Malcolm Gladwell contends that it takes ten thousand hours to become an expert in any field. That translates to about ten years of daily practice to become truly world-class (and very few people really have the time or dedication for that).

Luckily, Florida professor Anders Ericsson, the world expert on experts, says greatness doesn't have to take such an enormous amount of time. Having studied the best musicians, chess players, NBA shooters, and virtually everyone dramatically better than everyone else at what they do, he says the real key is to find the learning sweet spot that primes the brain to produce myelin[3].

Ericsson calls it deliberate practice, others deep practice. No matter the name, the formula is pretty straightforward.

How to get good at stuff (the not-so-secret formula):

1. Believe that you can learn (have a growth mindset) and be open to feeling incompetent.

2. Concentrate hard on a specific skill you are trying to master or improve (for example, a slice serve up the line in tennis).

> You need to isolate the exact element (which corresponds to a specific group of neurons) you want to strengthen.

3. Stretch outside of your comfort zone (give up just enough control) and expose yourself to the unknown.

Repetition inside your comfort zone has little use. Aimless hitting balls without a purpose is just playing around, but adding more power or more spin and making small adjustments will improve performance.

4. Get immediate feedback (preferably from a coach who can see what you miss) so you can correct your approach fast and can keep your attention where it's most productive.

You need to know whether or not you are getting better *while you practice*.

5. Practice the skill a lot.

6. Make a ton of mistakes and correct for them.

7. Practice more.

If you read any book on skill or talent, you'll find a similar formula. It seems practice doesn't make perfect, actually. Deliberate practice—practice that is designed—does. Sure, it's hard. It hurts. But it works. More of it equals better performance, and tons of it equals expert performance. Good luck!

☐ TOMORROW

☐ NEXT WEEK

☐ SOMEDAY

☑ NOW

Use it or lose it

If you don't continue to apply certain skills or knowledge, you will inevitably lose them over time.

Only connections and pathways that are frequently activated are retained. Other networks that aren't consistently trafficked such as the details of the Revolutionary War, or *Are You Smarter Than A Fifth Grader?* style questions, will be pruned or discarded so that active connections—what you're learning now or what's important in your current life—can become stronger. The brain doesn't waste real estate.

The idea of "use it or lose it" is also precisely why many scientists believe that mental sharpness declines as you age. As simple as it sounds, if you disengage and don't continue to stimulate and challenge your brain in later life, you will lose your edge. Alzheimer's, of course, is a different beast. Our understanding of the disease is muddled, and a cure is still far off. A growing body of evidence, however, shows that if you have normal brain matter and function, many cases of brain deterioration and aging are preventable.

The best way to stay sharp as a tack into old age:
- Exercise at least fifteen minutes a day
- Eat healthy
- Indulge your curiosity
- Take on new hobbies
- Learn new skills
- Stay socially active

CHAPTER
ATTENTION

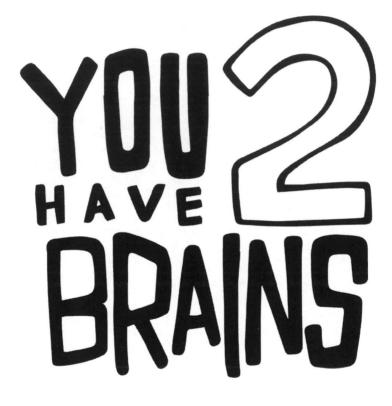

System 1, System 2

In *Thinking, Fast and Slow* by Daniel Kahneman—the only psychologist to ever win a Nobel Prize (in economics)—we discover that we have two brains. System 1 and System 2, for convenience.

System 1 is fast, instinctive, emotional. Primordial. Automatic. Subconscious. Intuitive. Associative. Biased.

It's at work when a musician plays her scales or when an NBA player shoots a free throw. When you have to calculate the answer to 3 + 3 in your head. Or when you make a left turn through an intersection.

System 2 is slow, deliberative. Rational. Calculating. Conscious. Analytical. Nuanced. Mature. It demands effort and attention.

It takes charge when you have to calculate the product of 17 and 25. When you're writing an essay. When you're trying to figure out what to order at a new restaurant. When you are immersed in a task.

When you engage in System 2 thinking, your pupils dilate. Your heart rate increases. You get angry if anyone or anything tries to interrupt you. Your vision narrows. According to Kahneman, this intense focusing "can make people effectively blind", which basically means don't try to calculate the product of 17 and 25 while making a left turn. It's impossible to do both at once.

System 1 and System 2 are constantly competing for control. System 1 usually wins; it is quick and the brain is lazy and likes to be on auto-pilot. Moreover, System 2 takes self-control, which is depleting and unpleasant to exert.

After years of science reporting, Winifred Gallagher came away convinced that she knew "the grand unified theory" of the mind—basically how to balance System 1 and System 2: "Like fingers pointing to the moon, other diverse disciplines from anthropology to education, behavioral economics to family counseling, similarly suggest that the skillful management of attention is the *sina qua non* of the good life and the key to improving virtually every aspect of your experience." Attention—that is, what we choose to focus on and what we choose to ignore—plays an important role in defining our quality of life. If you can police your mind, Gallagher says, you can improve your life.

When learning, constantly check in with yourself and don't be a slave to the automaticity of System 1. Its conclusions might arise out of misperception or illusion and can lead you astray.

Focused vs. mind-wandering mode

Since the beginning of the 21st century, neuroscientists have made great strides in coming to understand two modes of thinking that are critical for learning. We'll call them the focused mode (when you're highly attentive) and the mind-wandering mode (when your mind tends to relax and bounce from thought to thought).

The focused mode involves deep concentration and effort. It's turned on when you're solving a math problem, taking a test, or giving a presentation, and is associated with the concentrating abilities of the brain's prefrontal cortex, right behind your forehead! Concentrate intently on a task, and *bam*, you're in focused mode.

When you're in mind-wandering mode, your attention relaxes and your mind starts to drift. Your thoughts turn inward and become loosely connected. You might start thinking about the future or whatever else is lingering on your mind.

If a task is boring, the mind-wandering mode can hijack your consciousness—for instance, when you gloss over a page from your book and realize you have no idea what you just read, or when you're driving on the freeway and miss your exit because you were daydreaming. Because this mode is a spread-out network (not localized to a specific region of the brain or pattern of neurons), it is also what allows us to suddenly gain new insight on a problem we've been struggling with and is associated with "big picture" perspectives.

It turns out we toggle back and forth between these modes constantly, using one or the other. As a result, as long as you're consciously focusing on a problem, you're blocking the mind-wandering mode. What's fascinating (and we'll get to this later) is that mind-wandering insights often build on top of preliminary thinking done in the focused mode.

Our brains evolved to focus on one thing at a time

Psychologists have found that people can only attend to a certain amount of information at a time. According to a 2004 TED talk[1] by Mihaly Czikszentsmihaliy, that number is about "110 bits of information per second".

That may seem like a lot, but even simple daily tasks are cumbersome on the mind. Just decoding speech, for example, takes about 60 bits of information per second. That's why driving is so much more difficult when there's loud music playing or when there are friends in the car, and why when you're busy checking messages on your phone and your mom asks you "What did I just say?", you have absolutely zero clue.

According to engineering professor Barbara Oakley, the co-creator of the most popular online psychology class in the world, "Multitasking is like constantly pulling up a plant. This kind of constant shifting of your attention means that new ideas and concepts have no time to take root and flourish." Indeed there is a metabolic cost every time you switch tasks, which gradually wastes energy and drains your ability to stay focused.

Oakley's secret to uber-productivity: *do one thing at a time.* Reduce and eliminate distractions like a madman. Never add to the current workload or environment until you are ready to move on to the next task.

Our ancestors were expert single-taskers. They hunted, gathered, cooked, ate, talked, and slept—always one activity at a time. They didn't have Facebook, Twitter, email, news sites, blogs, or online forums to distract them.

From an evolutionary perspective, tens of thousands of years is an eye-blink. A sneeze. Not nearly enough time for significant improvements. You are no different than those who came before us. No matter what you tell yourself, *you cannot multitask better than you can single-task.*

The world is not the way you see it

The human brain has evolved to hide from us what we don't pay attention to. In other words, we often don't know what we're missing because our brain can completely ignore things that are not its priority at the moment—even if they are right in front of our eyes. Neuroscientists like to call this phenomenon *inattentional blindness*; a fascinating example is the basketball demo. If you haven't seen the video[2], view it now before reading any further. Your job is to count how many times the players wearing white t-shirts pass the basketball, while ignoring the players in black. Do your best to get the correct answer.

(Spoiler alert: if you haven't seen the video, reading the next paragraph will mean that the illusion won't work on you.) Because of the processing limits of your attentional system we just went over, following the players in white and the basketball, and keeping track of the number of passes, takes up most of the attentional resources of an average person. The rest are taken up by ignoring the players in black and the basketball they are passing. At some point in the video, a man in a gorilla suit walks across the scene into the middle of the players, bangs his chest, and then walks off. Most people watching the video don't see the gorilla. The reason? The attentional areas of the brain are simply overloaded. If I had asked you *not* to count the number of passes, however, you would have surely seen the gorilla.

If there is one thing I want you learn from this section, it's not to jump to conclusions. Our minds don't work the way we think they do. We think we see ourselves and the world as they really are (a philosophy known as naive realism[3]), but we actually miss a whole lot. We tell ourselves stories to help us make sense of the world. We create mental models of how things work and why people do what they do. We mistake what we believe for what is true. We reject what puzzles us and what fails to line up with our worldview. We see what we expect to see, and tend to miss things we don't expect to be there—the invisible gorillas of life.

Within our narrative—what we tell ourselves about how we got here, what our talents are, and what our priorities should be—we act in a way that seems reasonable. To be clear, the narrative isn't *true*. It's merely our version, our self-talk about what is going on.

Stamp this into your mind: there's always something you might be missing. Your reality is not the whole reality. Be open to multiple interpretations and multiple truths.

CHAPTER
MEMORY

Vast interconnections

Whenever you experience something, a unique network of neurons fires, like popcorn in a pan. Looking up at the Northern Lights? Visual centers that represent shadows, green, pink, and blue light up. That same skyline an hour later looks different, and so recruits an entirely different set of neurons to represent it. Watching a tennis match? Neurons fire for face recognition of the players, motion detection for the players, the ball, and the rackets, and visual centers that represent blue, green, and white light up. Higher cognitive areas keep track of whether or not the ball lands in bounds and what the score is.

Every thought, feeling, perception, and experience we have has a unique neural companion: if it didn't, we would perceive different ideas as the same. *It is precisely this difference in patterns of activity that enables us to distinguish concepts from each other.*

Additionally, each neuron can be part of many patterns of interconnection, just as each memory can be reached through many inputs. The memory of a special NBA championship game, for example, can be triggered by something as generic as the smell of a hot dog or as specific as the face of the person you were sitting next to.

How exactly a collection of cells could "contain" memories remains one of the hardest unsolved problems in neuroscience. For now, be content with knowing that when you remember something, you somehow bring the neurons involved in the original experience back online.

There is plenty of room

Consider these numbers. You have around a hundred billion neurons in your brain, and each of these neurons forms thousands of connections (or synapses) with other neurons. Mathematically, the number of possible patterns that can exist on even one thousand synapses is larger than the number of molecules in the universe, and each brain region will see only a tiny fraction of these possible patterns in a lifetime. Simply stupefying.

Because of this capacity to store information, many psychologists agree that nearly every conscious experience is kept somewhere in the brain—all the sights, sounds, smells, bike rides, and gross vegetables—and that the mysterious gray glob in between your eyes is a perfect recorder. The hard part is merely finding information and pulling it out again.

So then if it's all up there, why do we forget? As Patrick Jane of the Mentalist eloquently describes it, "Memory is unreliable because the untrained brain has a crappy filing system. It takes everything that happens to you and throws it all willy-nilly into a big, dark closet. When you go in there looking for something all you can find are the big obvious things, like when your mom died or stuff you don't really need. Stuff that you're not looking for, like the words to Copacabana. You can't find what you need, but don't panic because it is still there."

Many students say they can't possibly cram it all in their head, so they have to pick and choose, often forgetting important details. The issue, however, isn't space. *It's access.* The best learners find a way to organize information so that it can be retrieved quickly, efficiently, and reliably.

Am I the sum of my memories?

Your memory stores your personal experiences, how you feel about people, language, likes and dislikes, physical abilities, and everything else you know about the world. Without this miraculous ability to store and recall information—which tragically plagued a guy called EP, an amnesiac whose memory was so bad he didn't even know he had a memory problem—you would have no real feeling of self, no past to examine, learn from, or enjoy. You would be nothing.

Our thoughts and dreams, our plans and habits, our triumphs and experiences all remarkably arise from a three-pound mass (and all of its intricately associated electrical firings). When its activity stops, you stop. When it gets injured or comes in contact with a drug, your character changes in line. When it dies, you die.

With this knowledge, it's tempting to say, yes, you are the sum of your synapses. Unfortunately, memory is not as rich as you might expect. It is not a perfect video recorder. Your memory of who you were at sixteen is not the same as who you actually were at sixteen. The crazy college story you always tell at parties probably didn't go down exactly the way you portray. The groups of neurons that represent experience never activate exactly the way they did during the original event (which would make recall vivid and realistic), which makes memory more like watching a low-quality, incomplete replay that corrodes and warps over time.

A story we tell ourselves

Memory is fiction. I don't mean to say we deliberately lie or make up our memories; we truly believe we remember things clearly, but the mind is a funny, flawed object. What happened, and what we recall happened, are often two very different things.

In a 1995 film, British army captain Robert Daniell was interviewed about his experiences liberating the Bergen-Belsen concentration camp. He recounted how he was the first soldier to go into Belsen and how he saw empty gas ovens, which had been cleaned out because there was no fuel to run them—that's why there were corpses lying in piles six feet high. Daniell reported that "it is as clear to me now as it was then."

The only problem is that Belsen didn't have gas chambers.

Take a step back—most people would think a memory like liberating a Nazi death camp would leave an indelible print in the mind—it would be unforgettable. However, news of other camps and inaccurate popular media coverage managed to make the memory *false*.

I know it sounds like something concocted by the staff of *The Onion* but this phenomenon isn't unusual. George W. Bush is famous for his recollection of having seen the first plane hit the World Trade Center before he entered a Florida classroom. In reality, he had been told that a plane had hit the building (footage of the actual crash did not exist until months later). Similar accounts of where people were and what they were doing on 9/11 are woefully inaccurate.

It also turns out asking "How fast were the cars going when they *smashed* into each other?" versus *"bumped"* can influence how witnesses testify in court. In this scenario, a single word used to describe the collision seemed to better predict the estimate in speed than the speed itself.

Just because a memory is easy to retrieve doesn't mean it's accurate. Memory is not like a DVD player or a library. You can't just put in the tape or look up the call number for an event and reexperience it second by second, detail by detail. Our memories can (and often do) change over time. To crib a metaphor from cognitive scientist Daniel Levitin, remembering is like opening up a Microsoft Word file where that memory is stored and automatically opening it up to "edit".

Memory is not just a replaying, it is a reconstruction and a rewriting. It is quite like the game telephone. Each time you recall an event, your brain distorts it. The next time you remember your first day at school, you actually may be recalling information you retrieved about that event at some later time, not the original event.

No matter how good your memory is, you still have false memories. What *could* have happened becomes what you *wish* happened becomes what *did* happen. We can't help but let the present color the past. Be wary of overconfidence.

So next time you hear a politician make a false claim about what he remembers, keep in mind he might not be maliciously deceiving you. He might not even realize the memory is wrong (and if you tell him, he probably won't believe you).

MEMORY comes in different FLAVORS

Distinct categories

Scientists divide memory into categories based on the amount of time it lasts: working (really short), short-term, and long-term. Here are some helpful definitions before I try to explain how memory works in less than a hundred words.

Working memory

Every day we keep particular pieces of information in mind, briefly until we need them. Some examples: remembering a phone number between the time you hear it and the time you dial; figuring out a tip (the bill is $28.15, call it $30; 10% of that is $3, half of that is $1.50, add the two and you get $4.50, the 15% you were aiming for); holding driving directions in mind ("take the first left, continue for one mile, after you pass the hospital bear right, right at the stop sign, then it's the second building on the left—you can pull in the driveway"); looking at the board and analyzing various possible sequences of moves in a chess game; keeping the phrases of this sentence together as you figure out its meaning. Think of working memory as your mental scratch-pad (a temporary workspace that stores information so that you can access it quickly and perform computations as necessary). If you're into computers, it's your mental RAM. When tasks are done, you simply erase the mental blackboard and begin again with new information. The number of items you can hold in your working memory caps out at around seven (the length of phone numbers is not a coincidence), although some Einstein-type folks are known to have much higher capacities, which allow them to run more complex and sophisticated programs in their head. On a more hopeful note though, "normal" people can improve their working memory through deliberate practice.

Short-term memory

A place for holding what you just saw, heard, learned, etc. Unless rehearsed or repeated, its contents quickly decay over time (i.e. typically one to two days).

Long-term memory

Your brain's hard-drive, which permanently stores, manages, and retrieves information for later use.

Semantic memory

General world knowledge (facts, ideas, concepts, meanings and beliefs) that we accumulate throughout our lives and can access on demand. Having an idea of what a dog is and looks like. Recognizing color names. Knowing that America was attacked on September 11, 2001. Being fairly sure you shouldn't put a cat in a blender.

Episodic memory

Episodic memory is specific to each individual. It's the collection of autobiographical experiences (times, places, associated smells and emotions, and other contextual who, what, when, where, why knowledge). Remembering when you brought your first dog home from the breeder. Reminiscing about your first day of high school. Recalling where you were and what you were doing when you got your college acceptance letter.

Procedural memory

>Information about how to do things, like walking, talking, or shooting a three-pointer. It's commonly known as muscle memory.

Okay, here we go: working memory is where new information is stored and combined with old information. This is all thinking really is—you receive input from outside sources and that input is placed in your working memory and manipulated. In order to retain information, which is the ultimate goal of effective learning, you need to transfer information from working to long-term memory. This process is known as *consolidation*. Most information, however, especially content that is meaningless or only experienced once, does not not make it to long-term memory, and is instead discarded.

RELATE to what you ALREADY KNOW

The more associations, the better

"Memory is like a spiderweb that catches new information. The more it catches, the bigger it grows. And the bigger it grows, the more it catches."
- Joshua Foer

Being able to access any memory regardless of where it is stored is called *random access*. DVDs and hard drives work this way—you can jump to any spot in a movie or hard drive by "pointing" at it. Videotapes do not. To get to a particular scene on a tape, you need to go through every previous point first (*sequential access*).

Our ability to randomly access our memories from multiple cues is extremely powerful. If you're into computer science, it might help to view human memory as a kind of *relational database*.

Having relational memory means that if I want to get you to think of a police car, I can induce the memory in many different ways. I might make the sound of a siren, or give a verbal description ("a sedan used by cops to enable them to respond to crime"). I might try to trigger the concept by an association game, by asking you to identify what the Ford Crown Victoria, the Chevrolet Suburban, and the Dodge Charger all have in common (most people realize quickly that these are all common types of police vehicles). All of these things and more are *attributes* of the police car: its blackness, its emergency vehicle-ness, its speed, the fact that uniformed men and women drive it, that its doors are bullet-resistant.

If the end of that last sentence got you thinking about what other vehicles have fortified exteriors (for example, armed trucks at the bank or SWAT vans), you have discovered a fascinating concept: we can categorize objects into many, and seemingly infinite, ways. And any one of the cues we've discussed has its route to the neural representation of *police car* in your brain.

In addition to neural patches in the brain that represent attributes of things, those attributes are also connected to other things. A police car is black, but so are many things: ants, dress shoes, belts, tires, black Labrador retrievers—it's pretty easy to keep going. The reason you can think of all those objects easily is because when you think of *black*, you're sending electrical signals through the network and down the branches to everything else in your brain that connects to it, which even includes concepts associated with the color *black*, like darkness, evil and mourning.

A key to understanding the mind is that on its own, it doesn't organize things the way you might want it to. It's enormously powerful and flexible, but it's not like a library or your garage; you can't just put things anywhere you want.

People who say connections lead to learning don't go far enough. Connections *are* the learning. Surface learners focus on facts. Effective learners construct new knowledge by connecting new ideas to as many old ones as possible. They know that what we learn depends on what we already know—that you need a conceptual framework to embed what you're learning. It takes knowledge to gain knowledge. Seek not to memorize, but to reinvent and discover for yourself.

All you need to know is one thing: there's virtually no limit to how much learning we can achieve so long as we relate it to what we already know.

MAKE THE *meaningless* MEANINGFUL

Ms. Rider

Why do we remember some things better than others? Or (I know what you're thinking) why does memory seem random? To give a short answer, "It's probably not," asserts the director of UCLA's Brain Research Institute Gary Small. "It's just that most people don't always understand what makes one experience more memorable than another."

The seven rules for best-remembered experiences are as follows:

1. Is it *meaningful*?

Let's say you need to remember the serial code "2MBAEPA14". By themselves, the nine characters mean nothing; luckily they can be deconstructed into the number "2", "MBA" (a master of business administration), "EPA" (the Environmental Protection Agency), and then finally "14". You can easily remember this sequence by thinking of a man who spent two years getting his MBA (the standard time) and then went on to work at the EPA for fourteen years. Another illustration of the importance of meaning is a nifty idea known as the Baker/baker paradox, which goes like this: if I say to you, "Remember that there is a guy named Baker." That's his name. Then I say to your friend, "Remember that there is a guy who is a baker." A couple of days later, I come back and ask for the word I told you awhile back. Your friend will likely get it and you won't. How come? Because Baker doesn't mean anything to you. It is entirely untethered to other memories in your skull. But the common noun "baker"—we know bakers, the funny white hats they wear, the flour on their hands, that their stores smell good. And when we first hear the word, we start making these associational hooks, to make it easier to fish out at a later date. The entire point of remembering in everyday life is to figure out ways to transform capital B Bakers into lower-case B bakers—to take information that is lacking in content, significance, or meaning, and reinvent it so that it becomes meaningful in light of all the other things your mind has to keep track of.

2. *Relevant*?

It makes sense for us to remember useful information because it helps us survive and maximize our chances of success in a changing world. Of course, the definition of "useful" depends on how we were raised and what is important to us. What we think is useful now might also become useless later, and vice versa.

3. *Structured*?

The brain remembers best things that are repeated, rhythmic, rhyming (and alliterative). This is why songs, stories, analogies, metaphors, and mnemonic devices work great; they make the meaningless meaningful.

4. *Interesting*?

We are inherently curious. We like to learn about our favorite subjects and accumulate skill. Random, weird facts are cool, too.

5. *Distinct*?

Events that are unique (e.g. your twenty-first birthday, your brother's marriage, the first time you saw a giraffe) tend to be easier to remember because there is nothing to compete with them. On the other hand, I doubt you can remember what you ate for breakfast last Thursday, because there was probably nothing special about that Thursday or that particular breakfast, unless you had leftover pizza and spilled it on your shirt just before leaving the house for an important appointment.

6. Was *emotion* involved?

If something makes us incredibly scared, happy, sad, or angry—four of the primary human emotions—our brain releases chemical tags to make that memory more likely to stick. This makes evolutionary sense—emotionally important events are probably the ones we need to remember to survive (things like the smell of rotten food, the sound of an approaching predator, the friend who broke a promise). These chemical tags are exactly the reason we so readily and vividly remember the attacks of 9/11, our first kiss, and Donald Trump's election victory, but not the last trip to the laundry machine.

7. Is it *repeated*?

More rehearsals, more environments, and more contexts all lead to more connections and stronger memories.

CHUNK IT UP

Chunk it up

Chunks are pieces of information wrapped up into a meaningful whole. You can take the letters "N", "F", and "L" and bind them together into one conceptual, easy-to-remember chunk, "NFL", an acronym which evokes various images of Bud Light, violent sacks, and packed stadiums.

Similarly, you can take all steps required to safely get on the freeway and package them into one easy process—merge.

Other examples of chunks:
- Acronyms like NBA
- A completed puzzle
- Idioms like "Make yourself at home"
- How to find the x-intercepts of a function using the quadratic formula (by extension, the ability to understand and solve any specific kind of problem)
- "I'll get dressed" (one thought, multiple actions required)
- The concepts of global warming or continental drift
- The US Constitution
- Making a particular food dish (chefs have hundreds of chunked recipes and techniques)
- Hitting a forehand in tennis
- This book

Beginning readers often struggle with comprehension because of chunking (or rather lack of chunking). They're processing each letter and word very carefully, and their working memory simply can't comprehend what they're reading because it's overwhelmed by these individual units of information. As time goes on and someone becomes more skilled as a reader, they no longer have to think so carefully about what's in front of them—they're compressing the information into chunks of words they already understand.

Once you chunk up a concept or idea—once it becomes intuitive—you don't need to remember all the underlying details (the *what* becomes more important than the *how*), and since your brain has fewer pieces of information to process, it can run more efficiently and free up working memory for additional thinking.

To make this point even more clear, imagine yourself sitting at a game for a sport that you're very familiar with. You know what's going on because you understand the rules, what players can do with the ball (if there is one), and why players get penalized and for how long. This is all built out of chunks you've assembled about that sport. Each one of those chunks comes together to form a picture in your mind about how it should be played. If, however, you were to sit down and watch a sport you knew nothing about (curling comes to mind), you'd be at a loss. Since there was no context ahead of time, you probably wouldn't have any idea about why the crowd is either cheering or booing, or why a certain player is considered the best. If it's a sport that is similar to something you already know (rugby and American football are quite similar), you can probably put some things together about this new sport from chunks you have surrounding the more familiar one.

Learning a new subject follows a very similar pattern. If you don't know anything about mathematics, but jump right into learning advanced physics, you'll have no clue what most of the symbols mean and be completely lost. This is because the problems aren't going to explain the basic mathematical principles you need to know in order to solve them—you're expected to have that information in your mind ahead of time. Once you have the chunks you need, you can read that textbook and not only understand it, but maybe even glean some new insight that hadn't occurred to you before.

For centuries, chess has been regarded as the ultimate test of brainpower. Yet it's been proven that expert players, who can easily memorize boards after one glance, aren't geniuses, and I mean no major cognitive advantages. How could this be? Because they see the board differently, as game configurations rather than individual pieces, and lump up sequences of potential moves into distinct strategies. They retrieve from memory past situations that are similar to the current one and use that information to inform their decision-making.

What really differentiates experts from amateurs (across chess, music, cooking, math, sports, you name it) is the ability not only to call on a vast library of chunks within long-term memory, but also to draw meaningful conclusions about new data using all of the information they've consolidated over time. To put it another way, an amateur may very well have access to the same data, but he'll have trouble generating new, useful data without chunks to inform his reasoning. This is why many teachers have a hard time explaining concepts that are basic to them but new to their students. De-chunking your knowledge and explaining it to someone with little-to-no prior exposure is hard. For those established in their field, it can be a curse.

The bottom line is that you absolutely, positively, *must* have a firm library of chunks (knowledge) at your disposal before you can make progress in your learning. Anyone who tells you "knowledge is more important than facts" is wrong. The two are intimately connected. Memorizing key facts is essential to forming chunks and a lasting understanding. Advanced concepts are built on a few intermediate concepts, which are built on even more basic concepts. This is how the hierarchy of knowledge works. You must build on a base of simple concepts before working your way up to more advanced ones. There aren't any shortcuts here. Skip the foundation and you will eventually flounder.

How to make a chunk:
1. Make sure you're wholly focused on the information you want to chunk. No phone, no TV in the background, no thinking about the next social outing.
2. Drill down to the basic idea. Synthesize the gist. That said, understanding how something is done is not the same as mastering it. Do not confuse the aha! of "I get it!" with solid expertise. After your teacher explains something, review it shortly after and test yourself to see if you really know what's going on.
3. Gain greater context. When is this chunk used? When is it *not* used? Why? This will help you fit the chunk into the bigger picture and make it easier to identify errors when you make them (trust me, you *will* make errors, and that's a good thing). It will also facilitate applying this knowledge to novel problems and new environments, a phenomenon called *transfer*, which is critical to coming up with good ideas.
4. Review and practice the chunk. You must revisit to make sure it persists in your memory and can be accessed on command. Practice makes permanent.

EVEN the **BEST** use TRICKS

Those with exceptional memories are no different than you

A recent college grad, Joshua Foer lived at home with his parents while trying to make a go as a journalist. In 2005, he went to New York to cover a bizarre contest, the United States Memory Championship, where "mental athletes" memorize hundreds of random numbers, events, and dates, by looking at them just once. Decks of cards, lists of names and faces, and entire poems too.

Having an "average memory" himself, Foer thought that everyone participating was a freak of nature. He assumed their brains were unusual and somehow wired to easily remember copious amounts of information. He was jealous and *beyond* curious.

But the memory aces he talked to insisted that anyone, even Britney Spears, could do what they do. These people claimed that ancient visualization techniques (what Greek bards used to orate Homer's *Odyssey* from memory) were what enabled them to remember so quickly and easily.

A year later, Foer decided to come back to the same contest, but this time to complete—a sort of exercise in participatory journalism. Problem was, he won. The mental athletes were right—anybody could do it[1].

Foer is living proof that there are incredible memory capabilities present in all of us. Psychologically, we are still the same as our ancestors from two thousand years ago. Our brains are no smaller or less sophisticated. With motivation, focus, and a few clever tricks, we can all have excellent and worldly memories.

We must step back though. In the age of computers and smartphones, is memory even relevant anymore? Are there any drawbacks to replacing our own natural memories with new ways to record information externally (with paper, Post-It notes, note-taking applications, voice recorders, and so on)?

Yes, without a doubt. How we perceive the world and how we act in it are products of what we remember. No lasting joke, invention, insight, or work of art was ever produced by a Google search.

IMAGINE

Vision trumps all the senses

Russian Solomon Shereshevsky (S. for short) was a journalist in the 1920s. At that time in the Soviet Union, you did what you were told—nothing more, nothing less. Daily assignments were given out—explaining where to go, whom to meet, and what information to obtain. Everyone took notes, except S. When his editor asked him why, he recited part of the morning's lecture, word for word, and said he didn't need to carry around pen and paper, because he never forgot anything.

He was promptly sent to Aleksandr Luria at a local university for psychological testing.

Luria presented S. with hundreds of digits, complex scientific formulae, even poems in foreign languages, all of which he could memorize in a few minutes. Not only could he recite extensive lists of letters backwards, he could also remember them years later, as well as what clothes Luria had worn on the day he learned them. His memory appeared to have no limit.

Unsurprisingly, S.'s daily experiences were quite different from ours. His condition, known as synesthesia (which involves a blending of the senses), caused him to automatically translate the world around him into vivid mental images that lasted for years. If he was asked to think of a word or the number one, he would not only hear it, but see it, smell it, and experience a taste in his mouth and a feeling on his skin.

Unlike S., most of us are horrible at remembering names and phone numbers and long sets of instructions. That's because our ancestors never needed a vast memory for abstract symbols.

They did, however, need a memory for how to get back home from the week-long elk hunt, or for the location of a neighboring rival tribe on the rocky slopes to the north of camp. Here's what I mean: if I asked you to look around a house you've never been to before, you would soon get a sense of where the bedrooms and bathrooms are, the furniture layout, what's in the bathroom cupboard. In just a few minutes, you would acquire and retain thousands of pieces of information (and remember them for weeks if not longer). Our "where things are and how things look" memory systems are excellent.

When asked to describe what goes through their minds as they memorize, mental athletes recount a strategy that sounds almost exactly like what S. claimed was happening in his brain. Known as the memory palace, which dates back 2,500 years to ancient Greece, the idea is to populate a familiar place (such as your childhood home or local university) with images of the things you want to remember. This technique takes advantage of the fact that we have exceptional visual and spatial memories (that's why it's easy to imagine who might be in your kitchen right now or what your high school gym looked like). The more neural hooks you can build by evoking the senses, the easier it will be to recall the concept and what it means. The funnier, crazier, raunchier, weirder, stinkier, scarier, more bizarre the images—and the more senses involved—the better. You can find a step-by-step guide to forming a memory palace here[2]. A warning: the first time you do this, you will be slow. The speed and creativity needed will come.

CHAPTER
STUDYING

"Cramming seeks to stamp things in by intense application before the ordeal. But a thing thus learned can form new associations. On the other hand, the same thing recurring on different days in different contexts, read, recited, referred to again and again, related to other things and reviewed, gets well wrought into mental structure."
- William James, *Talks to Teachers on Psychology: And to Students on Some of Life's Ideals*

Preface

This chapter is practical; theoretical details are light. It is intended for those whose most pressing need is to become better studiers; to go from C students to B students or from B to A; who wish to learn the techniques first, and the why later (or never). It is for those who have so far found neither the time nor the means to dive deeply into neuroscience, but who want results and are willing to take the conclusions of science as a basis for action, without going into all of the specifics.

The following sections are some of the shortest in the book, but some of the most important. I expect that you will take the fundamental statements on faith, just as you would take statements concerning a basic law of physics if they were preached by Newton or Einstein. If you wish to know how the conclusions were arrived at, go to the Resources section and have your pick (or send me an email at lucas@beyondbrilliance.org and I can point you in the right direction); and if you wish to reap the benefits of decades of cutting edge research, read this chapter and do exactly as it tells you to do without hesitation.

Don't jump into the water before you can swim

Nail down the fundamentals first. If you blindly start working on the homework without attending class, reading the textbook, or learning from others who know more than you about the subject, you're going to waste time, get frustrated and, ultimately, flounder. Focus on the basic chunks first, before moving on to the details. Make this non-negotiable.

Retrieval is king

"If you read a piece of text through twenty times, you will not learn it by heart so easily as if you read it ten times while attempting to recite it from time to time and consulting the text when your memory fails."
- Francis Bacon

The knowledge that rereading textbooks is often labor in vain sends chills up the spines of educators and learners, because it's the number one strategy of most people, including up to 90% of college students in some surveys, and is central to what we tell ourselves to do when we learn. Unfortunately, it has three strikes against it:
1. It takes a long time.
2. It doesn't lead to durable learning.
3. It creates the illusion of knowing, where familiarity with the material is mistaken for mastery. When you have the book or your notes (or Google!) open right in front of your face, it's easy to convince yourself that the knowledge is in your brain. *But it's not.*

In order to learn well, you must *retrieve* (that right there is the single most important lesson in this book). This is true for anything the brain is being asked to remember and call up again in the future—facts, complex concepts, theories, and problem-solving techniques.

By attempting to *recall* material you are trying to learn, you create robust new memories and strengthen existing ones. This produces knowledge that can be retrieved more readily (and in more varied settings), and can be applied to a wider variety of problems. In practice, this means that as you're learning you should test yourself on the information you're absorbing. Even when you don't know something entirely, it's better to try and reproduce from memory than to give up early and look at the answer. *Active recall is always better than passive repetition.* Sure, it's more difficult, but it's undeniably more effective.

Space it out

"You can get a great deal from rehearsal,
If it just has the proper dispersal.
You would just be an ass,
To do it en masse,
Your remembering would turn out much worsal."
- Ulrich Neisser

When most people want to memorize something, they will generally reread, relisten or resay the information many times over a short period. While this method *will* work after a while, it's not the best, or even close.

Instead, what you should do is look at whatever material you need to study for a brief period, then wait a day to review it again. If you have no problem remembering the material, put it away again, but this time don't review it for two or three days. Each time you review the material and find you're still remembering it, increase the amount of time between reviews. The strategy I just described relies on practicing "a little bit here, a little bit there"—short review sessions, spaced out over a significant chunk of time, at least two weeks before the exam—to cement material into the mind using sturdy neural bricks that won't break down on test day.

Spaced repetition, as it's called, is very much like watering your lawn three days a week for thirty minutes, instead of once for ninety. You're not working any harder or spending any more time (in most cases you actually need *less* time), but the impact is profound. *No other technique comes close in terms of immediate, noticeable, and reliable results.*

Embedding new learning in long-term memory, in which material is given meaning and connected to prior knowledge, is a process that unfolds over hours, and often days. By spacing out your practice, you let some forgetting set in (making it harder to recall concepts), but the effort required and the time periods between sessions vastly increase the strength of the relevant memories.

"So what is the optimal interval to wait before studying something again?" you might ask. Well, you want a little forgetting to set in, so the next session requires effort, but not too much forgetting so you have to fully relearn all the material.

In 2008, UCSD professors analyzed twenty-six different study schedules and actually settled on an optimized distribution[1]. In short, if you want to know how to best split up your sessions, you need to decide how long you wish to remember something. The most widely spaced, longest schedule is the most effective. With longer spaces, you forget more, but you find out what your weaknesses are and you correct for them. You discover which associations, which cues, which hints are working and which aren't. And if they're not working you come up with new ones.

Get comfy with Anki

So then if we know spaced repetition is the best way to learn, why do so few students use it? Why hasn't it caught on? Because it's hard to implement. Humans are forgetful creatures—it's hard enough remembering when the test is.

Luckily, in the age, we have *Anki*[2].

Anki is an intelligent spaced-repetition flashcard program which automates all of your review. This means that instead of going through terms and concepts in the same order every time, you see them at strategically spaced intervals, just before you would forget them. These intervals are based on how easy the card is for you to remember (you choose "easy", "medium", "hard", or "very hard") and how many times you've reviewed it before.

Because it's incredibly efficient, you can either spend less time studying, or greatly increase the amount you learn, or both. It's also free and has built-in cloud backup. The mobile applications for both iPhone and Android don't hurt either.

Since *Anki* is content-agnostic and supports images, audio, videos, mathematical markup, and custom formatting, the possibilities are endless.

You can use the program to:
- Learn foreign language vocabulary
- Study for the LSAT or MCAT
- Memorize anatomical parts
- Sharpen your geography
- Master long formulas
- Review key trends throughout history

Many people, upon discovering *Anki*, decide to download other people's decks to avoid the trouble of making their own. But this is essentially doing the opposite of what flashcards are designed for. The information in those decks is unknown to you and lacking context, so it is practically worthless. Alternatively, you should make cards out of information that is both relevant and interesting to you. By doing this, you'll leave a lasting imprint on your memory since the cards are going to contain chunks that you've personally selected. You also get a certain degree of quality control by making your own cards, since other people's decks may contain inaccurate, confusing, or incomplete information.

Again, the most effective way to use Anki is to make flashcards yourself (as you're learning a subject). It sounds like the hard way, but in the long run you'll save yourself a lot of wasted time by making cards that are personally relevant and that you'll remember beyond the course.

Stay on top of the material. Review every day. Make it a habit.

More great tips from an *Anki* master[3]:
- "Why?" questions are better than factoids
- Add images whenever possible
- Some like to organize their decks by subject and subtopics, but it might be better to use only one deck. That way, you're mixing everything together and making interdisciplinary connections more frequently.
- Make your cards two-ways. Instead of just having X on the front and then the definition of X on the back, add the reverse to your deck.

- Don't make flashcards for unimportant things or information you already know (it's not going anywhere).
- Flashcards are best used for learning things you want to be able to retrieve *immediately* (they aren't the best for hierarchical or "big picture" concepts)

If you're anti-technology and/or don't have access to a computer or smartphone, you can create a box system with index cards. Each box is labeled for a specific time interval, and you move the index cards from one box to another as you go through your reviews. For more information on how to do this, look up the Leitner system[4].

Change up the environment

"The idea of this remarkable piece of household stuff had so mixed itself with the turns and steps of all his dances, that though in that chamber he could dance extremely well, yet it was only when that trunk was there; he could not perform well in any other place unless that or some other trunk had its due position in the room."
- John Locke

Many public speakers choke because they never practice on the stage they are going to be using, or even in front of people. They enter a new environment and totally blank, because what made them comfortable, what helped them remember the flow of the presentation in their practice environment is no longer there.

By reviewing in new environments, what you know becomes increasingly independent of your surroundings. This doesn't mean you should constantly go to different libraries or spots in your house just for the sake of it (that will only waste time). But it *does* mean you should review on your way to class, on the bus, or whenever you have a spare ten minutes. Sometimes aloud, sometimes quietly. Sometimes with music, sometimes without.

Most importantly, if you have a chance to use the actual room you are going to be testing in (especially for a practice test), take full advantage. Cues in the room will work in your favor on the big day.

Constantly give yourself mini-tests

"There are known knowns; there are things we know that we know. There are known unknowns; that is to say, there are things that we know we don't know. But there are also unknown unknowns—there are things we do not know we don't know."
- Donald Rumsfeld

Testing in and of itself is a powerful learning experience. It is a chance for you to demonstrate your knowledge, changes and adds to what you know, and also dramatically improves your ability to retain material, by strengthening and stabilizing the related neural patterns and chunks in your brain.

The *testing effect* (what scientists unimaginatively call this enhancement in knowledge gained from testing), occurs even if test performance is bad and no feedback is given. Yes, the simple act of taking a test (no matter how poorly you do) makes a difference—truly remarkable. Of course, when you self-test, you'll want to get immediate feedback, so you can see what you need to focus on and adjust your strategy going forward.

Weaker students tend to grossly overestimate how well they understand material. As a result, they don't study much; they take the exam and believe they have done really well, and then are stunned when they find out they did poorly (because going in they didn't know where their gaps in knowledge were).

Don't fall prey to this trap by simply telling yourself you know the material. Mastering the lecture or text is not the same as the ideas behind them. Quiz yourself (as early and as often as possible) for proof of understanding—otherwise you won't know the things you don't know.

Mix up your practice

Most of us believe learning is better when you approach a topic with single-minded purpose: the *drill-and-kill* mentality that's supposed to burn a skill into memory.

Almost everywhere you look, you see examples of this kind of *massed practice*: two-week programming certifications, weekend continuing education seminars for professionals, and one-week sports camps to keep athletes sharp over summer.

In math textbooks, each section is dedicated to a particular kind of problem, which you study in class and then practice by doing about twenty examples for homework before you move on. The motto is: don't practice until you get it right, practice until you can't get it wrong. The next section has a different type of problem, which you learn and practice. On you march, section by section, through the semester. Until the test comes, and (oh no!) all of the problems are mixed up! You stare at each problem and ask yourself "Which technique do I use? Was it in chapter 6 or 7?"

That's because massed practice is easy. If the top of your homework says "Quadratic Formula", you just use it, without asking why. You don't have to consider "What kind of problem is this?" so you can select the appropriate strategy to use, *because you already know*. This is why word problems are hard, because few explicitly state which technique needs to be used.

As opposed to massed practice, which leaves students fuzzy on the basics and quick to forget recent material, you should study related concepts or skills in parallel, a technique called *interleaving*.

Surround new stuff with older stuff, to build. This strategy is harder and you'll feel like you're learning less, but you'll actually get better and longer-lasting results. Prepare your brain for the unexpected by giving it the unexpected. The surprise will generate deeper processing of information so when the test comes you know how and when to use a certain strategy.

In interleaving, it's crucial that you don't move from a complete set of one task to a complete set of a different one. You might think 100 forehands, followed by 100 backhands, followed by 100 volleys is mixing it up, but it's not.

The general goal of practice is to transfer to a game. A game situation is random, the skills needed at any one time change. So instead of doing 100 forehands, then 100 backhands, then 100 volleys, *practice like you play*. Do two backhands, then a forehand, then a backhand down the line to approach the net for two volleys and an overhead. If you practice like you play, you'll play like you practice.

If you know it, move on

Continuing to study or practice something after it is well understood is called *overlearning*. An example might be a student correctly solving a certain kind of math problem and then immediately doing several more problems of the same kind. Or keeping the training wheels on after you've learned to comfortably ride a bike.

Continuing to hammer away at something once you have it down does no good. If you know it well now, you'll know it for the test. You should instead start interleaving your practice with different material or different techniques. In math and science, this is crucial because just knowing *how* to use a particular problem-solving technique isn't enough—you also need to know *when* to use it. Randomizing different problem types and skills is the best way to develop this intuition.

STUDYING doesn't have to be SILENT

It does matter if Mom is listening

I didn't make up that header. Children who explain the solution to a problem to their mom (or to themselves) learn better[5].

"The basic idea is that it is really effective to try to get kids to explain things themselves instead of just telling them the answer," says Vanderbilt psychology professor Bethany Rittle-Johnson. "Explaining their reasoning, to a parent or perhaps to other people they know, will help them understand the problem and apply what they have learned to other situations."

Indeed teaching someone else what you know forces you to justify how you know it—to explain why a certain fact is true or why a concept works. It requires breaking down and simplifying chunks, and then repackaging them for others, which improves your own understanding and recall. It's hands-down, by far, the best way to learn *deeply*.

Even if there's no one willing to listen to you, you can (and should) use this strategy of explanation and elaboration. Find a quiet room where you can talk aloud, and talk! There's absolutely no reason studying has to be a silent process.

Raise your hand immediately

One of the best ways to reduce study time is to eliminate your question marks on the spot.

Here are four ways you can do this:
1. Ask questions during class.
2. If number (1) makes you feel uncomfortable, talk to your professor briefly after class.
3. Get answers from your classmates (especially the A students).
4. Come prepared to exam review sessions, where the most common problem isn't too many questions, but too few.

We've all heard the advice: if you're confused, it's almost certain others are too. *But it's true.* It's always true, no matter how you feel in the moment.

Don't worry about looking dumb. Worry about being dumb. Ask questions! Otherwise, when you finally get around to studying, you'll have unanswered questions, and you can't always ask your textbook for the answers.

A team sport learning is

(Yes, you are supposed to read that header in a Yoda voice.)

Virtually every academic activity in school is done solo. Worksheets. Homework. Exams. Presentations. Essays. Lectures might seem like they involve multiple people, but they too are primarily one-way. The teacher says something; the students furiously write down every syllable; there might be a question or two here and there.

In the real world, this would never happen. No competent waiter says, "I'm not sure what's in this dish, but I'll figure it out myself." No experienced salesman says, "Jeez, I don't really know how to quote that deal, so I'll just make up a price myself." Similarly, no academic researcher or military general or successful lawyer works alone.

Yet in school, isolation is the creed. If you study with others, you clearly can't cut it on your own.

This is baffling because all sorts of teams have to make a living out of learning together:
- Sports teams
- Performing arts troupes
- Scientific research groups
- Business executives

There is no reason academics can't be the same. Working together should be the norm. Group projects. Presentations. Lab reports. All of it.

So, go find a study partner (or two or three). Explain things to each other. Correct each other's mistakes. Fill in the gaps in each other's knowledge. Send each other study guides. Do practice problems together. Leverage the power of the group.

Sometimes you won't have a choice. The material will be too difficult to tackle alone. In that case, you've probably picked a course of study that will pay off.

TREAT EVERYTHING as TEST PREP

Treat everything as test prep

Many students believe that the only way to prepare for a test is to study. They go through the motions, learn next to nothing, and then release an ungodly amount of stress chemicals to cram a few days before the exam.

Stop for a second and think. It shouldn't be a surprise that everything you do before the big day counts, too. Lectures, reading, documentaries, projects, talking to peers, homework. HOMEWORK. Otherwise they wouldn't exist. Of course there are exceptions—some assignments are objectively nothing more than busy work—but generally these components of a course are necessary and helpful.

So if you're the type of person who approaches assignments with an "I need to get this done" attitude, stop. Treat every lecture and assignment as an opportunity to learn and slowly make your way to mastery. If you stay on track this way, studying for exams will be less daunting, more straightforward and take less time, since you will have a durable foundation to build off of when you actually begin review.

Always prepare for an essay exam

In 1914, a professor in Kansas invented the multiple choice test. Yes, it's only about a hundred years old.

There was an emergency. World War I was ramping up, hundreds of thousands of new immigrants needed to be processed and educated, and factories were hungry for workers. The government had just made two years of high school mandatory, and we needed a temporary, highly efficient way to sort students and quickly assign them to appropriate roles.

In the words of Professor Frederick J. Kelly, "This is a test of lower order thinking for the lower orders."

After the war, as President of the University of Idaho, Kelly disowned the concept, pointing out that it was an effective way to test only a tiny portion of what is actually taught and should be abandoned. The industrialists and the mass educators revolted and he was promptly fired by the university administration.

Kelly never intended to make his baby the gold standard. Yet the SAT, still the single most important filter and determiner of a student's progress, is still based on Kelly's lower-order thinking test. Same with just about everything, from No Child Left Behind exams to tests for medical and law school admission. The reason is simple. Not because it works. No, we do it because it's easy and keeps the massive train of students moving forward.

So what am I trying to get across? Well, it's straightforward. Doing well on a multiple choice test is a poor indicator of whether or not you know the material, since familiarity with the answer choices is often more important than understanding the nuances of the question.

So, do yourself a favor. Assume every exam will require you to write, to explain your reasoning, and to prove that you actually know what you know.

Focus on the underlying concepts. Build a holistic picture. Use recall. Practice your responses. Know more than you're expected to know, and you'll never have to worry about tests again.

CONNECT the dots DON'T collect them

Connect the dots, don't collect them

In *Civilization*, Niall Ferguson writes:

> A survey of first-year history undergraduates at one leading British university revealed that only 34 percent knew who was the English monarch at the time of the Armada, 31 percent knew the location of the Boer War and 16 percent knew who commanded the British forces at Waterloo. In a similar poll of English children between 11 and 18, 17 per cent thought Oliver Cromwell fought at the Battle of Hastings.

He laments the fact that kids only remember the greatest hits of history, recognizing the names of Gandhi, Martin Luther King, and Hitler, but none of the minor characters.

I say, "So what?" Who cares? I can't imagine a situation where knowing who commanded the British forces at Waterloo would help society. Anybody can look that up on Google. It's trivia. Yes, I said it, trivia, and much of what is taught in school is exactly that.

When access to information was limited, we needed to load students up with facts. Now, in an always-connected world, we can look up facts whenever we need them and in some cases faster than we can retrieve them from memory. *For free.*

"On the other hand," claims Seth Godin, "understanding the sweep of history, being able to visualize the repeating cycles of conquest and failure and having an innate understanding of the underlying economics of the world are essential insights for educated people to understand."

To be as clear as possible: it's not about the facts, it's about understanding. It's about the big ideas, the patterns, the consequences, and the parallels to modern day.

The industrial model of school is organized around exposing students to ever increasing amounts of stuff and then testing them on it. Collecting dots. Almost none of it is spent on teaching them the skills necessary to connect dots. *And the magic of connecting dots is that once you learn the techniques, the dots can change but you'll still be good at connecting them.*

CHAPTER
TESTING

Ignore those with the so-called "testing gene"

Everything comes easy to them. They don't study much. They ace everything. We all know people like this.

What to do about them: accept that not everything comes as naturally to everyone and move on. Getting jealous won't help. Instead, ask for their secrets—most of these seeming geniuses aren't actually that much smarter than everyone else, they just know how to manage their time and remain calm under pressure (both of which are teachable skills).

Why people choke and how to avoid it

A brilliant student fails an easy test; a savvy executive blows a key presentation; a star actor messes up his final lines.

Choking. We all know what it is and we've all experienced it.

When you feel the need to get everything right, to exert control over each small detail, sometimes it all comes crashing down. Why? Sian Beilock, the world psychology expert on screwing up in high-pressure situations, gives us three causes:

1. You thought you knew it, but you actually didn't.

> The illusion of knowing: the misjudgment that because facts or formulas or arguments are easy to remember right now, they will be tomorrow or the next day. It's the primary culprit in below-average test performance. Not anxiety. Not stupidity. Not unfairness or bad luck. It's the scenario when most of the questions seem to ring a bell, but when you are actually forced to search your long-term memory and come up with the answer or a solution yourself, you totally blank. *Never forget that mastering the lecture or text is not the same as the ideas behind them.*

2. You didn't know what to expect.

> This is very common and almost always avoidable. Each teacher has different topics she emphasizes, different formats for tests, and different standards for grading. You, and only you, are responsible for knowing what those are. If figuring them out is not your highest priority, then you should not expect to receive an "A" and you should work toward a more attainable grade.

3. You fell for the tricks.

> You weren't careful. You accepted the first answers that came to mind without double-checking and asking if they really make sense[1]. You let System 1 take over.

Assorted additional tips:

- Approach the exam as an opportunity to show how much you've learned, not as a chore. Tell yourself you are nervous because you are excited and really want to do well (which is often the case), not because you are afraid of doing poorly.
- Scan the whole test first, so you know what's coming and how long each section will take.
- If you blank, skip the question and come back to it.
- Don't panic when other students turn in their exams. *There's no trophy for finishing first.*
- If you really start to feel the nerves build (which can be crippling especially when pressure is high), ask if you can take a twenty second walk outside. It'll help you relax and regain your composure.

Failure is nothing more than a gap

"If you hit a wrong note, it's the next note that you play that determines if it's good or bad."
- Miles Davis

Failing an assignment or a test or even a class doesn't mean you're incompetent. It means you didn't do what you needed to do this time. Maybe you skipped a few classes, or maybe you really were a model student who showed up, took notes, studied hard, and it still didn't work out. Either way, it's solvable.

Failure is merely a gap. It shines light on inaccurate pictures of reality—things you think you know that just ain't so—and strategies that don't work as expected. You didn't fail because you're stupid or powerless or unworthy. You simply didn't perform this time around, and there's nothing inherently wrong with that. You can always learn your way out of trouble.

So next time you fail, or get anything less than you want, a simple attitude change from "I'm stupid!" to "Wow, I wasn't prepared this time. I need to adjust my approach." or "Hmm, I'm surprised I got that wrong. That's really interesting. I want to figure out why." will do wonders.

Ask yourself:
- What happened?
- What did I expect?
- What specific mistakes did I make?
- What can I learn from the gap?

If the only reasons you can come up with are "I didn't work enough" or "I don't have the testing gene", check out Richard Felder's "Memo to Students Who Are Disappointed With Their Last Test Grade"[2]. Go through the checklist. Thoroughly. If you're not ticking many boxes, you can bet there's something you can fix for next time. For more pointers, go to your teacher or professor. He'll gladly help. It's his job.

CHAPTER
PROBLEM SOLVING

Being confused is normal and necessary

There's this notion in school that if you don't know how to do something, you're simply not good at it. Brilliant students, in particular, have trouble dealing with confusion—they take it as proof that they can't cut it on their natural abilities. They shy away from challenges, for fear of getting the answer wrong and being labeled an imposter. But the learning process is all about overcoming confusion and working through difficulty—for each misstep makes your brain a little stronger.

We all start out the same: small, helpless balls of mass. We spend about a year unable to walk, and about two more before we can articulate our thoughts. Gradually, we learn to read and write, and swim and dance, and eventually feed and fend for ourselves. How? By failing, falling, trying, experimenting, and struggling, and then failing some more—but we get there.

Remember, nothing is intuitive at the start, but know that even if you haven't gotten it *yet*, there's nothing stopping you from understanding it soon. Failing is the gateway to learning. Keep struggling. Keep growing. The power of "not yet" is mighty.

WORK

OUT

OF

ORDER

Hard first, then jump to easy

The classic way students are taught to approach problem sets and tests is to tackle the easy problems first. That way, by the time they finish the simpler problems, they'll have the confidence to handle the hard ones. This strategy works for some people, mostly because, well, anything works for some people. For others, however, it's counterproductive, since tough problems require lots of time and scream for the power of the mind-wandering mode.

So which strategy is better? The answer is to start with the hard problems and then quickly jump to the easy ones. The steps for this technique are:
1. When you first get a problem set or test, first scan to get a sense of what it involves.
2. Then start with the hardest problem.
3. If you get stuck or sense you might not be on the right track, pull away and switch to an easier problem.
4. Repeat step (3) if necessary.
5. After finishing an easy problem, switch back to a hard problem.
6. Continue to switch back and forth between easy and hard until you finish the assignment or test.

When you return to the harder problems, you'll often find that the next step or even the solution is more obvious to you. By using different parts of your brain to work simultaneously on different thoughts, in a sense, you're being like an expert chef. While waiting for the steak to sear, you can swiftly chop up some fruit for the salad, turn to season the soup, and then stir the sizzling onions. Using this method on tests ensures that you will have a little bit of each problem finished, which is especially important if your instructor gives partial credit. It also helps you avoid a concept called *Einstellung* (which we'll get to next section), by forcing you to look at a problem from multiple perspectives. The only trick is that you need the discipline to pull away from a problem once you find yourself stuck for a minute or two. Otherwise, if keep working on the same problem, you might find that the solution only pops into your head after the test, since once you gave up and shifted your attention, the mind-wandering did the little work needed to finish the job.

BE...
PATIENT

Take breaks to get unstuck

One of the most fascinating (and potentially crippling) concepts in psychology is called **the Einstellung effect**[1]. It manifests when you have an idea in mind, or a simple initial thought, that prevents you from finding a better idea or solution. (The German word *Einstellung* means "installation"—you can remember this by imagining your brain *installing* a roadblock that prevents you from making progress because of your initial way of looking at something).

The *Einstellung* effect is a frequent stumbling block for students. It kicks in when your first intuition is misleading, so you plod along, never getting closer to the actual solution because you're on the wrong path. In this scenario, when your focused mode prevents you from seeing any other course of action but the one you're taking—or maybe the problem is so tough you don't even know where to start, or what it is asking—you should:

1. First, ask yourself if you've jumped into the water before you could swim. Do you have the fundamentals nailed down? If not, this is a recipe for failure, and you should return only when you've established a better foundation. If yes, move on to step (2).
2. Stop and take a break. Engage the mind-wandering mode and allow your attentional resources to replenish.

General mind-wandering mode activators:
*   Nap
*   Jog or walk (preferably through an area with lots of green)
*   Swim
*   Dance
*   Play a sport
*   Go for a drive
*   Draw or paint
*   Take a bath or shower
*   Listen to music, especially without words
*   Play an instrument
*   Meditate or pray

Best If used briefly, as rewards:
*   Video games
*   Surf the web
*   Talk to friends
*   Read a relaxing book
*   Text friends
*   Watch Netflix

Once you distract yourself from the problem at hand, the mind-wandering mode has access and will continue to search for an answer unconsciously. What a deal—you can keep learning even while taking it easy. When you return, you'll often be surprised how quickly and easily the answer pops into your head. And if you're still stumped, you'll often be further along in your understanding.

Figuring out a difficult problem or learning a new concept almost always requires one or more periods where you're not consciously thinking about the problem. Be patient. If you really can't get unstuck, ask someone for a different perspective or advice on how to take the initial steps; however, it's better if you first wrestle with the problem yourself *before* requesting help—having some basics down will make you much more receptive to an explanation.

CHAPTER
CREATIVITY

Start early, then stop

Almost a hundred years ago, Russian psychologist Bluma Zeigarnik noticed that a waiter had better recollections of unpaid orders. After everyone had paid, however, he was unable to recall any more details about the orders. In a series of follow-up experiments designed to uncover the underlying phenomenon[1], Zeigarnik discovered that incomplete tasks tend to dominate our attention. That's why being interrupted when you're almost finished with an email is extremely annoying—you can't stop thinking about pressing "send"—because our brains crave closure.

For messier, more difficult items like essays, lab reports, and final projects, you can use the Zeigarnik effect to your advantage—by quitting before you're ahead. *This is the only time in this book when I'm going to suggest you procrastinate, so listen carefully.* An interesting thing happens when you quit: your mind gets angry. It subconsciously scans for cues in the environment, breaking fixed assumptions. It tunes itself to see and find pieces of information related to your work (things you normally wouldn't pay attention to), because it *needs* resolution. It needs to finish.

Sometimes the only way to make an essay or a project better is to actively procrastinate, letting your mind unconsciously collect ideas and material to use once you're back at work. Start as soon as possible, and then take frequent breaks for inspiration until you gradually make your way to the finish.

There are no new ideas

In 2011, Brian Uzzi and Ben Jones, business professors at Northwestern University, analyzed a range of creative academic papers. Using a computer algorithm, they evaluated 17.9 million papers and found that in the most creative ones 90% of the content had already been published somewhere else[2]. The best papers were considered groundbreaking not because they developed brand new concepts, but because they took existing ideas and put a fresh spin on them.

Creative doesn't have to mean original. Innovation and invention actually thrive on reusing and building on top of the old. Johannes Gutenberg combined the ancient technology of the wine screw press—for squeezing juice out of grapes—with his knowledge of metallurgy to create the first printing press. Gunpowder was originally used as a treatment for skin diseases and as an insecticide, until the Chinese military began experimenting with the substance in the 8th century B.C. Teflon—what slick, non-stick pans for cooking pancakes are made of—was originally created in 1938 and sold to the U.S. Government for use in artillery shell fuses and in the production of nuclear material. In fact, no scientist today would be able to produce new knowledge in his field if he couldn't stand on "the shoulders of giants" (as Stephen Hawking would say)—men such as Darwin, Newton, and Tesla—for foundation and inspiration.

Lucky and random connections (often across disciplines) drive serendipitous discoveries and new applications. A great example is the German chemist August Kekulé: centuries ago, he dreamt of a serpent eating its own tail, and suddenly discovered how carbon atoms could arrange themselves in a ring to form the molecule benzene, which is now used to make dyes, detergents, drugs, plastics, and pesticides, and is also a major part of gasoline.

It's easy to think that subjects like English, math and history are all separate—in school we move from one subject to the next—but in reality they're all interconnected. Physics wouldn't exist without math. Learning a foreign language teaches you the specifics of English grammar, and helps you learn a third language even easier. Doctors prescribe their patients drugs, which wouldn't exist without chemistry. Politics and economics are joined at the hip. Being able to read, write, and deal with people well (psychology!) are critical skills in business. Learning a little bit of neuroscience and physiology can improve your fitness and sports game. And history (which isn't just a bunch of random facts) reminds us of how we got here and helps us avoid making the same mistakes our ancestors did.

As we can see, it's no surprise that some of the most creative and productive minds ever—Aristotle, Da Vinci, Einstein—all dipped into many different disciplines. As you move through school (and life), keep reminding yourself of the way things are connected, of their relatedness. Always be looking for ways to take what you learn in one context and apply it to another. The neural mechanism for "this is kinda like that" is everywhere in your brain.

So take that class you've always thought was interesting but doesn't count toward your major; you'll find a way to employ it someday.

INSIGHT follows the PAUSES in life

Welcome boredom

Boredom. We spend most of our youth trying to avoid it. It makes us feel uncomfortable, so we scramble to find something to do to lighten the uneasiness.

In today's world, we're close to eradicating it completely. Got five minutes to spare? Whip out your phone for a glance at your Twitter timeline. Have a bit more time? Check Instagram and Snapchat. Another moment? Memes.

With all-day smartphone access to news, sports, games, gifs, everything we could ever want, there's no reason to be idle anymore—sounds positively wonderful! Unfortunately, if you're keeping yourself stimulated every possible second of every day, you're missing out on the benefits of being bored. Yep, I said it: boredom can be good—it's not just a source of pointless pain. It's actually a signal to our brain that we are not doing what we want to be doing and a push that motivates us to come up with new ideas—a clear asset to creativity.

Ironically, the harder you push your brain to come up with something creative, the less creative your ideas will be, and the more you focus on a specific solution, the more it will elude you. So I'm going to give you some advice I doubt anyone has ever given you: if you get bored and stop making progress on difficult creative work (essays, lab reports, presentations), embrace the struggle and let your mind wander. Turn off the TV and take an Internet sabbatical. Retreat from the world of busyness. Fully disconnect. Go for a long walk, not to be like Thoreau in order to underscore some complicated social critique, but to experience firsthand the practical benefits of giving your mind a vacation. Of course that's not an excuse to be lazy (being undriven is vastly different than purposefully deciding to be quiet sometimes), but see where your mind takes you and what it solves in offline mode. Crucial insight often comes after abandoning a task, when you're not deliberately thinking about it.

CHAPTER
PRODUCTIVITY

Self-control is limited and depletes fast

People fight desires all the time. Not surprisingly, sleeping, eating, and sex are the most common. But also in the top ten, according to psychologist Roy Baumeister, are "taking a break from work...checking email and social networking sites, surfing the web, listening to music, and watching television"—things students do all the time.

In multiple experiments, Baumeister found that adults who are distracted and forced to make many choices throughout the day eventually lose their ability to resist desire. *Your self-control, in other words, is not a function of your character that you can deploy without limit; it's instead like a muscle that tires or a gas tank with a finite amount of fuel.* Over time, distractions drain your pool of willpower until you can no longer resist temptation. The same will happen to you, regardless of your intentions—unless, hopefully, you are smart about your habits.

The key to developing productive habits is to move beyond motivation—I'm sorry but you won't always be motivated—and add *routines* to your life to minimize the amount of willpower you exhaust and the amount of choices you need to make on a daily basis.

The best way to preserve willpower is with *precommitment*, which means assuming your future self will be lazy and figuring out *now* where you're going to be and what you're going to wear, eat, and do at later dates. That way, when the time comes around you'll already know what you need to do and be confident that that's exactly what you should be doing.

It's also important to stay well fed while you work—your ability to resist temptation depends heavily on blood sugar[1]. This is an often-overlooked factor in why fat people who go on a diet have so much trouble. In order to resist eating unhealthy foods, they need to exert willpower. But, in order to have adequate willpower, they need to eat. Gnarly Catch-22!

According to Baumeister, who has tracked thousands of students over the course of their lives, *self-control is without question, by far, the best predictor of college GPA (and future success).* Not SAT score, not IQ, *not effort.* Self-control. Master your impulses and you can master anything.

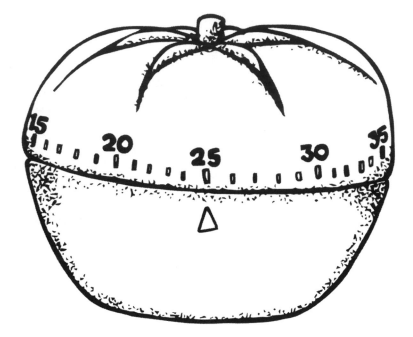

The little red tomato that started a revolution

Are you in the market for something easy to use? Fun to do? That will immediately improve your productivity? Obviously.

Here's how it works:

> Set a timer for twenty-five minutes. Close Facebook and Twitter. Turn off all notifications. Work. No interruptions or distractions whatsoever. Once time is up, take a five minute break. Feel free to check social media or talk to friends. Walk around. Go to the bathroom. Get some water. Have a snack. Do an organizational chore.

That's it. Deceptively simple, right?

This proven and popular time management hack, called the Pomodoro technique, from Italian *pomodoro* (tomato), has won the hearts of millions.

Why you should use it?
- You'll get more done. Working in short, intense bursts beats eight-hour sessions any day.
- You won't burn out, as it's virtually impossible to push yourself too hard with this method.
- There's a built-in reward every thirty minutes.
- Managing distractions becomes a piece of cake.
- You can repeat for as many cycles as needed.

If you feel like twenty-five minutes isn't enough to gain momentum, you can do fifty minutes on, ten minutes off—same results.

Note: If you use Google Chrome, add the Strict Workflow extension[2] to your browser for an easy-to-use online timer.

PROCESS NOT PRODUCT

Focus on process, not product

If you find yourself avoiding certain tasks because you dislike them or because they make you feel overwhelmed, here's a great way to reframe the situation. Focus on *process*, not *product*.

Process means the flow of time and the actions associated with that flow of time—as in, "I'm going to spend thirty minutes watching lectures" or "I'm going to spend an hour working on my essay".

Product is an outcome, something tangible—for example, the essay that is due tomorrow morning that you've waited the past two weeks to start.

To prevent procrastination, you need to avoid concentrating on *product*. The *product* is what triggers the pain and the discomfort that causes you to put assignments off.

Instead, learn to prioritize the building of processes and habits that will coincidentally allow you to knock out the unpleasant tasks. Focus on the small chunks of time—the Pomodoros— you need over days or weeks, to finish problem sets or prepare for tests. Who cares if you don't finish whatever you're working on in that twenty-five minutes? What's important is that you calmly put forth your best effort for a short time, inching your way to the finish line.

By focusing on *process* over *product*, you allow yourself to stop judging yourself (am I getting closer to finishing?) and just relax into the flow of work. This approach keeps you working when you're supposed to be working, and provides plenty of breaks along the way.

WHEN YOU WORK,
WORK HARD
WHEN YOU'RE DONE,
BE DONE

When you work, work hard. When you're done, be done.

The best students work differently. When they say they are going to study, they *actually* study. When they show up to do a problem set, they *actually* do the problem set. And when they sit down with a cup of coffee to write, they *actually* write. No email, no Snapchat, just work. Everything is planned and scheduled, ahead of time. They have morning routines, to automate that portion of the day and conserve willpower. They learn constantly and in blocks; even fifteen minute rest periods between classes are allocated for review. When they work, they turn off everything and are laser-focused—with full knowledge that (amount learned) = (time spent) x (intensity of focus). They work on single tasks for a long time without switching, allowing them to maximize their performance output. They try to structure their lives so that whatever they are doing *right now* is the best possible use of their time. Then, when they finish (which is usually early), they are free to play and do whatever they want for the rest of the day. Additionally, when they are sick or feeling off, they don't push. They stop working and let their bodies recover.

The worst students go to the library with only a vague idea of what they are going to work on and for how long. Consequently, they half-work, which means *constantly distracting themselves* with memes on Reddit or infotainment sites, and then ultimately leaving many hours later without having gotten much done. They use busyness as a proxy for productivity, and as a result waste much of their valuable time. When exams rolls around, they cram, staying up multiple nights in a row to make up for not having learned what they were supposed to have learned in stages. They perform OK, but not great. The cycle repeats.

The difference between great students and poor students: great students do what they say they are going to do. They don't lie to themselves. When they work, they work hard, and when they're done, they're done.

Transform distant deadlines into daily ones

Attack your workload bit by bit. Convert big projects into smaller, easily achievable tasks that show up on your daily to-do list. Plan where and when you are going to tackle them. Will you go to the library tomorrow afternoon? Will you leave your phone behind and go into a different room of your house this evening? Planning how you will implement what you need to do will make you far more likely to succeed in each task.

Decide what you are going to do each day the night before. Figure out when you'll work and for how long. When you go to sleep, your dreams will latch onto the big ticket items and begin working on them.

A look into my system: For managing tasks, I use *Trello*. I have labels for "Today", "This Week" and "Next Week" which I update as necessary. Anything more than two weeks out goes into "Later". "Next" is for quick fifteen-or-so minute tasks I can do before class starts or while I have a break. "Someday" is for items that I'd like to get to at some point but aren't critical right now. For scheduling, I use Google Calendar to visualize all my classes, to-do items (which automatically import from *Trello*), appointments, work sessions, and (most importantly) free time.

What's also important is that you decide how you'll work once you start—you'll need rules to stay on track. For instance, you might ban Internet use entirely, or create a metric such as words produced per twenty-minute interval to keep your concentration sharp while writing an essay. Without this structure, you'll find yourself again and again questioning whether you're putting in enough effort or working on what you should be, and these are dangerous drains on your willpower reserves.

Another technique many students and professionals use is what's called *the grand gesture*. The concept is simple: by radically changing your normal environment, coupled with perhaps investing a significant chunk of money and effort, you can increase the perceived importance of a task. To finish *Harry Potter and the Deathly Hallows*, for instance, J. K. Rowling locked herself in a five-star hotel room to do nothing but write. With that much money on the line, you can bet she didn't procrastinate or lose motivation. So, drive twenty minutes away to a coffee shop and *work*. Plan a full day out of boring tasks. The psychology of committing so deeply to the day's workload will force you to get it done (quickly). If you're running out of time or pressure is high, this tactic works especially well.

Will you sometimes need to make changes to your plan because of unforeseen events? Of course. But, remember, a little organization goes a hell of a long way. Keep your eyes on the prize, and don't get too frazzled by the occasional roadblocks. One step at a time.

WHERE you are NOW

vs

WHERE you want to BE

Where you are now vs. where you want to be

"Today I will do what others won't, so tomorrow I can accomplish what others can't."
- Jerry Rice

A powerful technique in motivation is called *mental contrasting*. In this approach, you think about where you've come from and where you are now and you contrast that with what you want to achieve. If you're trying to get into medical school, for example, this entails imagining yourself as a doctor, saving lives and making enough money to pay for your kids' college education. Once you've got those pleasant images in mind, *contrast them with the real, mundane aspects of your current life*—the endless trips to the library, the week-old leftover ramen on the table, the mountain of student debts.

Let's talk more about goals. We all have them, and we all want to achieve them (in a timely manner). Here is the formula that mathematically guarantees success:
1. Fix in your mind exactly what you want to be/do/have.
2. Decide what you are prepared to give in return (you will never get something for nothing).
3. Select a definite date by which you will have become this new person or done this deed or acquired these possessions.
4. Prepare a definite plan and begin to implement it immediately.

Now, based on the first four steps, write down a clear statement of what you want, the time limit for its acquisition, what you are prepared to sacrifice, and your plan for accumulating it. Read this statement aloud every day. This is the method of putting the subconscious mind to work for you through repeated suggestion. It will concentrate your mind on your burning desire until your subconscious mind accepts it as the inevitable and starts to devise ways of bringing it about.

Post pictures or words around your study and living spaces to remind you of where you want to be and the dream of where your studies will take you. Look at them when you're lacking motivation or making excuses. You'll feel a fire under your ass.

Go with the Flow

You've felt it before: full focus, full involvement, peak performance.

You're energized. You have no idea what time it is (and you don't care). Nothing can distract you, not even hunger or thirst.

The science world calls it *Flow*. In colloquial terms, it's when you're "in the zone". When you feel your best and you perform your best.

It's a state of heightened creativity, increased performance and accelerated problem solving. Absolute awareness, no effort. You're productive, and you don't even have to try. It's like a river current carrying you downstream, and it's critical to learning complex topics.

Many scientific breakthroughs have emerged out of Flow states. Same thing with significant progress in athletics and the arts.

In a ten-year McKinsey study, top executives reported being five times more productive in Flow[3]. Imagine being able to come in on Monday, take the rest of the week off, and still get more done than the rest of your peers.

Steven Kotler, co-founder of the Flow Genome Project, says we spend about 5% of our working hours in Flow. If that number could be nudged to just 20%, we could double our productivity.

My Flow hypothesis: the ability to get into Flow is becoming increasingly *rare* (since technological distractions are everywhere) at precisely the time it is becoming increasingly *valuable* in society. Consequently, the few who cultivate the skill will thrive.

So, the obvious question: how do I get more Flow out of my life? Well, good news: it's hackable, and it's a proven path you can take toward increased focus and accelerated learning.

Here are Kotler's main suggestions:

Occasionally ignore habits and routines.

> Automatic pilot is efficient and saves energy, but it doesn't help with Flow. So, shake things up. Even brush your teeth with the opposite hand.

Pay attention with all your senses.

> Learn by doing and experimenting. Engage as many sensory streams as you can.

Keep a journal.

> Figure out the triggers that launch you into Flow.

For a full in-depth course, check out Kotler's Flow Fundamentals[4]. It ain't cheap ($497), but it's a "Zero to Hero" program!

CHANGE X
see what happens

——————————————
REPEAT
——————————————

CHANGE X
see what happens

Self-experimentation is the key to a better you

Self-experimentation—doing something different for several weeks and observing the changes—can be used by non-experts to (a) see if the experts are right and (b) learn something they don't know.

Your experiments, to begin with, should center on procrastination. Keep notes on when you don't complete what you intended to complete and why. Figure out what cues throw you off your discipline. Text messages? Social networking? Email? Sometimes the answer might be as simple as location—crowded libraries don't work well for everyone. In addition, pay careful attention to times of the day when you have high/low energy and focus (and find learning easier/more difficult).

In *The Now Habit*, Neil Fiore suggests keeping a detailed daily schedule of your activities for at least a week to identify your problems areas. By logging your reactions, you can slowly start to apply the pressure you need to change your response to distraction and temptation. Although there are many different ways to monitor behavior, keeping a written log is critical if you want to make real changes.

After you tackle procrastination, you can use the same three-step formula—(1) change one thing (2) document the results (3) adopt or reject the change—to launch self-experiments on sleep, energy levels, mood, weight—really anything you want— to hack your way to a more productive, new and improved you.

Technology tips: the best apps and programs for studying and getting work done

Timer
- The Pomodoro technique: www.pomodorotechnique.com
- Tomato Timer: www.tomato-timer.com

Flash Cards and Studying
- Anki — intelligent flash card software that is highly customizable, an excellent spaced repetition algorithm: www.ankisrs.net/
- Quizlet — millions of existing study decks on the web or on your phone, interactive games and practice tests, collaborate with friends: www.quizlet.com
- StudyBlue — flash cards, notes, and study guides: www.studyblue.com

Tasks and Planning
- Google Tasks and Calendar
- Todoist: www.todoist.com
- Trello — excellent for group projects and delegating tasks to multiple people: www.trello.com

Note-Taking
- Evernote — my favorite piece of software, note-taking, recording random pieces of information, clipping web pages for offline reading, decluttering paper around the house, storing pictures and other files, excellent search function that helps you find practically anything. You can also set reminders on notes for review: www.evernote.com
- Jumpcut — Have you ever cut and pasted two or three things, and lost a hugely important thing that you cut first? This tool, which is free, allows you to store (and easily retrieve) 40+ copied or cut things from your clipboard. Only for Mac (www.jumpcut.sourceforge.net). PC alternative (www.ditto-cp.sourceforge.net).
- Microsoft OneNote — organize thoughts, to-do lists, and projects: www.onenote.com

Document Storage and Collaboration
- Dropbox — access your files from anywhere, on any device, and share them with anyone: www.dropbox.com
- Google Docs — create, edit, and collaborate on documents, spreadsheets, powerpoint presentations, and more (all online): www.docs.google.com

Declaring War on Procrastination
- Brain.fm — music to focus, relax, or sleep (does not work for everyone): www.brain.fm
- Freedom — cuts off your access to the internet during the times you specify, blocking access to email, Facebook, Twitter and a multitude of time-sucking websites. Works on iPhone, iPad, and Mac and and Windows: www.freedom.to
- Rescue Time — tracks time spent on applications and websites, giving you a picture of how you spend computer time: www.rescuetime.com
- Spotify — work to music or white noise: www.spotify.com/us
- StayFocusd — limits the amount of time you can spend on time-wasting websites: Available on Google Chrome Web Store
- Write or Die — helps eliminate writer's block by providing consequences for procrastination and rewards for achievement: www.writeordie.com

Easiest Way to Stay Focused
- Disable all notifications on your computer and smart-phone

CHAPTER

SLEEP

You snooze, you win

Students are obsessed with sleep deprivation. The longer you're awake and the longer you study, the more you are a hero. The more you are encouraged to brag. The more your peers respect you and think you are on the path to success.

Unfortunately, sleep is like a bank account. Avoid overdrafts and your credit history will be perfect. Accumulate debt, however, and there will be compounded interest and an uphill battle to recover. There may even be an enduring little red flag marking your "bad sleep" credit history. You might not get a loan when you need it.

Most people (especially students) vastly underestimate sleep's impact on their performance. But the costs of deprivation are heavy and accumulate quickly. With insufficient sleep you become anxious, irritable, and confused. Memory is impaired. Creative solutions that help you get things done fast and easy are hard to come by. Morale also plummets, causing you to engage in less-demanding tasks like browsing Facebook, chatting with friends, or reading yet another Buzzfeed article that doesn't matter; the motivation needed to tackle important tasks is simply not present.

Sleep has been a topic of research for over a hundred years; we know volumes about it. We know it is essential for learning and memory, as much of the encoding required to lock information into long-term memory occurs during sleep, where neurons active during learning become active again (this repetition likely plays a role in strengthening connections between neurons, thereby solidifying the associated memory). We also know that adequate sleep *before* learning grants major memory advantages.

Your ability to regulate your emotions similarly hinges on sleep, as deprivation frequently causes irritability and extreme mood swings (by amplifying the fear and stress circuits in your brain). Many actors actually take advantage of this fact by staying up all night to prepare for scenes where they need to be angry or volatile.

Sleep is also critical to creativity and insight (many major scientific discoveries were the product of dreams), warding off infections, metabolic regulation, and the efficiency of your glymphatic system—your brain's waste management provider—which removes excess fluid, toxins and other debris while you doze.

Simply put, sleep is essential to success as a student. This is why I always try to get about eight and a half hours. Seems to be the perfect amount for me. Some might need more—those under twenty-five should be getting around nine. Some less. But don't think you're special. Claiming that you can get by on less than six hours is an illusion—one that is hard to bust and will eventually bite you in the ass.

Once in awhile, you might need to pull an all-nighter. That's ok. Understand the consequences and don't make it a habit.

Being tired is not a badge of honor. So get more sleep. Stop bragging about how tired you are, and access your peak potential.

A short doze goes a long way

When your eyelids can barely open, it's impossible to do your best work. Instead of powering through or crushing caffeinated drinks to stay awake, take a short nap (Thomas Edison's secret tool for creativity and self-improvement[1]). Aim for 10-20 minutes max. You'll get a full cognitive reboot and wake up feeling great. It's often better than caffeine or exercise. Even seven minutes is enough if you're really short on time.

Since there is actually a biologically hardwired dip in alertness in the middle of the day in all humans, the best time to nap is between one and three in the afternoon. Any earlier and you might have trouble falling asleep. Any later and it might interfere with your nighttime routine. Try to keep it short. A nap lasting thirty minutes or longer is more likely to be accompanied by sleep inertia, which makes you groggy and cranky.

For extra alertness, try a "caffeine nap". Down a cup of coffee, Red Bull or other caffeinated drink and fall asleep for fifteen minutes; the caffeine takes time to kick in and won't affect the quality of the nap. You'll wake up extra sharp and without the urge to keep snoozing.

If you plan on staying up late and need to ward off sleep deprivation, ninety minutes is best. That'll take you through a whole cycle.

If falling asleep during the middle of the day is difficult for you, find a dark room, ideally cool. Use one of those eye masks you get on plane rides. Minimize noise. You won't have trouble.

Napping is not for the lazy and unambitious, or solely for old people with nothing better to do with their time. Napping is for anyone who wants a better memory, a longer attention span, heightened creativity, fewer mistakes, and reduced stress and anxiety.

Don't be like the rest of your sleep-deprived, espresso-craving zombie peers. Nap!

Routine is key

Our internal body clock is extremely sensitive. It cycles almost exactly every twenty-four hours and is influenced by many environmental cues such as light and temperature. Support your body's natural rhythm. Pick a schedule that works for you and stick to it:

- Go to bed and wake up at the same time.
- Avoid sleeping in. Messing with your schedule on weekends especially is like experiencing jet lag twice weekly. It wreaks havoc on the brain and body.
- Expose yourself to bright sunlight in the morning.
- Nap, but be smart (doze too late or for too long and falling asleep at night can be extremely difficult).
- Consider getting a sleep app with a smart alarm—it'll go off during the light sleep stages, when your body is naturally ready to wake up. *SleepCycle* and *SleepBot* are top-downloads. They also have a variety of extra features to help you track and optimize your sleep.

At night:

- Avoid bright screens. If you like to work late on your computer, download an app called *f.lux*[2] to get rid of the harmful blue light emitted by your screen. If you need to use your phone, turn the brightness down.
- If you like to read, paper is better than an e-reader.
- When it's time to sleep, make sure the room is completely dark. Also make sure nothing in the room is emitting light. Even the numbers on your alarm clock can disrupt sleep.
- Keep your room cool. 65°F is ideal.
- Minimize noise (I suggest getting a nice pair of silicone ear plugs).
- Make sure your bed is comfortable.
- If you get up at night to go to the bathroom, keep the lights off. You'll fall back asleep faster.

Relaxation techniques are a great way to unwind, calm the mind, and prepare for sleep. Some simple ones include:

- Reading
- Listening to soft music
- Light stretching
- Meditating
- Taking slow, deep breaths
- Progressive muscle relaxation. Start with your toes. Tense everything as tightly as you can. Then relax. Work your way all the way up to the neck.
- Visualize yourself in a peaceful, serene location

Other tips:

- Get regular exercise
- Avoid caffeine after 3 p.m.
- Avoid alcohol before bed. You might fall asleep faster but sleep quality will be poor and you'll wake up feeling groggy. If you're drunk, it's actually better to stay up, let the alcohol wear off, and skimp on hours.
- Have a cup of herbal tea before bed.
- Make a list of things to tackle tomorrow so they're not swimming around in your head all night.
- If it's been more than fifteen minutes and you can't fall asleep, get up and do something relaxing and non-stimulating. Return to bed only when you're tired again.

CHAPTER
LANGUAGES

THERE IS NO LANGUAGE LEARNING GENE

Lessons from an Irish polyglot

You are either born with the language-learning gene, or you're not. Pure luck, right? At least, that's what most people believe.

Enter Benny Lewis. For years he was atrocious at learning languages. He was the worst in his German class in high school, spoke only English into his twenties, and even after spending six whole months studying abroad in Spain, could barely muster up the courage to ask where the bathroom was in Spanish.

His frustration with conventional methods eventually led him to take a different approach, as described in his book and website *Fluent in 3 Months*.

According to Benny (who is now fluent in over ten languages and conversational in many more), the following language-learning rules are "must-know":

Learn the right words.

Many people cite a bad memory for new vocabulary, so they quit before they even start. But you don't need to know every word of a language to speak it. You don't even need to know half of them. For example, in English just one hundred words make up 50% of all words found in written material. Step it up to three hundred words and you can master approximately 65% of all publications. This pattern persists in every other language. Always start with the most commonly found words and then branch out from there[1].

Cognates are your friend in every single language.

Cognates are "friends" of words you know from your native language that mean the same thing in another language. For instance, Romance languages like French and Spanish have many words in common with English. Nation, precipitation, communication, and thousands of other *-tion* words are spelled exactly the same in French, albeit with a different pronunciation. In Spanish, *-tion* simply becomes *-cion*. Many languages also have words that share a common (Greek/Latin or other) root, which might be spelled a little differently, but are extremely hard *not* to recognize, such as *medicina* (Italian) or *Ingenieur* (German). To find these common words in your target language, simply search for "[language name] cognates" or "[language name] English loan words".

The best resources are free.

Surprisingly, Rosetta Stone and other expensive books and courses aren't the best. On his website, Benny has a comprehensive list of language-learning tools (many free) that he and others have vetted[2]. I suggest you try out several and see which ones work for you.

Adults can actually be better language learners than kids.

A common myth: *I'm too old to learn a new language.* While we do know that your native language refines your ability to hear the particular sounds of your language, and worsens your capacity to hear the sounds of other languages, no study has ever shown that adults can't learn a new language. In fact, under the right conditions, grown-ups are actually better learners than their younger counterparts because they can intuitively figure out unknown grammar rules[3]. The real reason many adults fail at learning a new language is because they have escape routes. Babies don't. They have to learn or else they'll never know what is going on. They also aren't afraid of making mistakes or being judged.

Use mnemonics.

How most people learn lists of words in school: the classic *repeat-repeat-repeat* method. For example, if you wanted to learn that the Spanish word *bailar* means to dance, you would say aloud "Bailar...to dance...bailar...to dance...bailar...to dance..." perhaps a dozen or even a hundred times with the hope that it will eventually stick. But sometimes no matter how many times you try to remember what a word means, you just can't seem to burn it into memory. This can be extremely frustrating, especially when you forget a word you know you've heard dozens of times. An often effective solution to this problem is to use a mnemonic designed to aid memory. For example, "My Very Educated Mother Just Showed Us Nine Planets" is the mnemonic I always used to remember the order of the planets in the solar system. With languages, a mnemonic should consist of a funny, silly or otherwise memorable pattern of ideas, letters, or associations to help make a word "stickier". With *bailar*, you could use the fact that *ballet* (similar spelling) is a form of dance, which helps you make the right association. Although this technique might seem tiresome, it actually saves time in the long run. My advice: have fun and use your imagination!

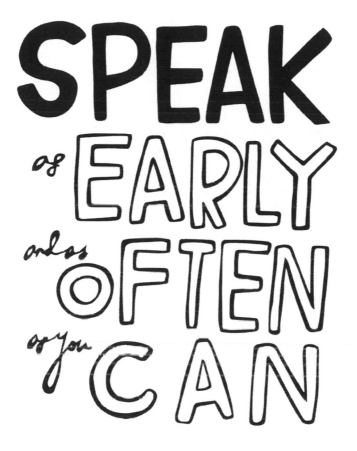

In order to learn a language, you need to live it

Over half of the world speaks more than one language. In Europe, most people actually speak three or more comfortably. And in Luxembourg, the language of instruction actually depends on the subject being taught. Math and science use French, while the rest use German.

This means that speaking only one language is a cultural, not a biological, result. So when adults who only speak English fail at learning a new language, it's not because of their genes or other such excuses. It's instead because *the system they are using to learn is broken*.

If you truly want to accelerate your language learning, you need to depart from traditional classroom methods (which center around memorizing vocabulary and grammar, only a small part of the picture) and adopt these principles:

Speak as early and as often as you can.

There's a misconception that once you learn all of the vocabulary and grammar of a language, you then know that language. Unfortunately, that's not how it works. The problem is that you can never really "learn" a language, you just get used to it. A language isn't something that you know or don't know, it's a *means of communication between people.* Learning a language isn't spending months or even years memorizing lists of words and learning grammar. It's speaking and using the actual language, which most people NEVER actually do. And not being in a country that speaks your target language isn't an excuse either. You can use *Italki* to find natives interested in talking to you, and to schedule a free Skype call that automatically handles time-zone issues. The site can also help you find excellent and affordable one-on-one instructors.

Embrace mistakes.

Using a language is about communication, not perfection. Sure, you could wait until you are ready to say "Excuse me kind sir, what are your favorite Italian restaurants in the neighborhood?" but "Italian food where?" conveys the same basic information. You will be forgiven for your directness; it's obvious you are learning. Perfect mastery is a useless goal anyways. You don't know every word of English, but that doesn't stop you from using it. You will never be "ready". So go out on a limb and talk to natives—they will appreciate you for trying and will often give you helpful feedback. Make mistakes. Tons of them. Look stupid. Laugh. Be enthusiastic. Keep progressing.

Translate your world.

Even if you can't travel, find a way to immerse yourself. Listen to radio shows or podcasts in your target language. Read foreign magazines and news articles. Change the language on your phone and social media accounts. Put sticky notes on everything in your house with the names for those objects. If you use Google Chrome, download the Language Immersion extension[4] which translates parts of the web page you're currently viewing into one of sixty-four languages supported by Google Translate. Scrolling over a translated word or phrase lets you hear it pronounced, and clicking a translation turns it back into your native tongue. Even though the translations aren't perfectly accurate (Google Translate is still learning), this is one of the best ways to build your vocabulary and learn pronunciation. The tool even has novice, intermediate and fluent settings, depending on how much of the page you want translated.

Always be reviewing.

According to a 2012 study[5] of Duolingo, the world's most popular application and website for language learning, "a person with no knowledge of Spanish would need between 26 and 49 hours (or 34 hours on average) to cover the material for the first college semester of Spanish." That's only twenty minutes a day, for three months. The lesson here: you don't need to be in class to learn a language. Instead of checking Facebook or Twitter during your breaks, spend five minutes reviewing your Spanish.

DECONSTRUCT

SELECT

SEQUENCE

STAKES

The method of DiSSS

Tim Ferriss has spent most of his career studying the ins and outs of learning. He's the author of three New York Times best-selling books and runs a top podcast[6] where he uncovers the tactics, tools, and habits of the world's most elite performers.

A polyglot himself, he speaks five languages proficiently (English, Mandarin, Japanese, German and Spanish) and has experimented with over a dozen others. His framework revealed below:

Deconstruct

Before you waste hundreds or even thousands of hours on a language, you should deconstruct it. Ask a native speaker: what are the most important blocks to start with? what are the rules I need to know before proceeding? what are the most common mistakes beginners make?

Start with a few simple sentences.
- The banana is yellow.
- It is Sam's banana.
- I give Sam the banana.
- We give him the banana.
- He gives it to Sam.
- She gives it to him.
- She does not give it to him.

These seven sentences alone expose much of the language. You'll learn if and how verbs are conjugated. How to use negation. Fundamental sentence structure: is it subject-verb-object (SVO), like English ("I eat the banana"), is it subject-object-verb (SOV), like Nepalese ("I the banana eat"), or something else? What are the noun cases? All from just seven sentences.

Here are two more:
- I want to give the banana to him.
- She must give it to him.

Select

Which 20% of the blocks should I focus on for 80% of the outcome I want? What verbs are most common? Nouns? Phrases? Can I just stick with the present tense, or do I really need to learn the past and future as well? Compress this information. Make a one or two page cheat sheet that you can refer to, especially if study starts to get overwhelming.

Sequence

In what order should I learn the blocks? In what order should I practice them? It makes no sense to memorize complex verbs before you have a handle on basic ones like *to eat* and *to drink*. Start with the easy, then build.

Stakes

How do I make sure I actually follow the program? If there's no incentive, there's no penalty for failing. No cost. No judgment by your peers. No matter how thorough your plan, you are probably terrible at self-discipline (we all are). You need weekly goals. You need ramifications that will hurt if you don't follow through. Ferriss recommends *stickK* which lets you put your money on the line: if you don't follow your program, your wager will go to an anti-charity, an organization you despise. You'll also have a referee (usually a friend) to keep you honest.

This is how Tim Ferriss learns, and he does it better than nearly everyone else on the planet. With that said, there is no one best method to learn a language. Find something that is effective for you. And, above all, experiment!

CHAPTER

TIPS, TRICKS, AND HACKS

Exercise is the best learning drug

"Methinks that the moment my legs begin to move, my thoughts begin to flow."
- Henry David Thoreau

Our bodies and brains were built for moving—long distances per day[1]! So get up and take a walk right now. I'm serious. Just for a few minutes. Or do a wall sit. I promise you will feel better. As I write this, I'm actually about to leave the basement of the Berkeley Law School, my usual writing spot, and get a breath of fresh air myself.

According to doctor John J. Ratey, the world's foremost expert on the mind-fitness connection, physical exercise:

- Gets more blood to the brain, bringing it glucose (aka sugar) and oxygen for energy
- Stimulates serotonin, dopamine, and norepinephrine circuitry (these are all essential for paying attention and help spur positive emotions)
- Elevates levels of a protein called BDNF (brain-derived neurotrophic factor) which stimulates the growth of new neurons in the hippocampus
- Enhances learning and memory and promotes new connections between neurons
- Helps stave off the usual withering of tissue

If these bullet points and the finer points of exercise (which are far beyond the scope of this book) intrigue you, please take some time to at least skim Ratey's new book *Spark*[2]. The evidence is incontrovertible. Elevating your heart rate and breaking a sweat can help you battle stress, strengthen memories, and physically remodel your brain for peak performance.

So, if you're already an avid exerciser, congratulations. You're two steps ahead and have already granted yourself a wonderfully effective "life hack." If not, get up and MOVE. Make it a daily habit. No need to be crazy if the gym isn't your thing. A few push-ups, pull-ups and squats is all you need. Maybe some running. Or swimming. At least twenty minutes a day. Find a partner for motivation. No more excuses.

Nourish the machine

Low energy breeds procrastination. You space out. You check your email. You start talking to friends. Under these mental conditions, getting anything done is nearly impossible.

Here are five simple rules for maximizing energy and concentration:

1. Drink water constantly.

Hydration combats unhealthy food cravings, wakes you up, and keeps you feeling good and functioning properly. So get a Nalgene bottle, post up near the drinking fountain, and start chugging. Don't worry about having to go to the bathroom so much (for context, I piss like a racehorse when I study)—frequent walks stabilize alertness and help engage the ever-so-important mind-wandering mode we've discussed before.

2. Monitor caffeine and sugar intake carefully.

Too much caffeine or sugar will make you overstimulated and unfocused. Not enough and you burn out fast. Find the right balance and don't overdo it. If you're a coffee drinker, for example, start off strong and then switch to decaf or tea before you pour another cup.

3. Treat food as energy, not reward.

Food is a source of long-term energy, not a coping mechanism. Processed carbohydrates, sugary drinks and fast food provide a quick energy boost, followed by a crash and increased cravings. Stick to fruits, vegetables, anything whole grain, lean meat, and nuts to keep your energy levels stable for long periods of time.

4. Boost your brain and promote growth.

Diet plays a key role in maintaining brain health and creating new cells. The following have a direct effect on brain dynamics.

Enhance brain function:
- Green tea (slows mental decline)
- Blueberries (reduces inflammation in the brain and boosts memory)
- Dark chocolate (improves blood flow and protects the brain against free radical damage)
- Omega-3 fatty acids (keep neurons functioning at optimal speeds)
- Beets (increase blood flow to your brain which improves mental performance)
- Antioxidants (protect neurons against damage)
- Flax-seeds (an excellent source of alpha Linolenic acid (ALA), a healthy fat that boosts cortical function)
- B-vitamins (help neurons burn glucose for energy)

Decrease and/or damage brain cells:
- Saturated fats
- Processed foods and sugars
- Nicotine (in excess)
- Alcohol (in excess)
- Chronic stress

5. Don't skip meals.

Even on the busiest of days, eat regular meals. Hunger robs you of your energy and ability to focus. And snacks aren't enough to make up for the corresponding low blood sugar. Don't make your stomach cranky.

Meditation (or sitting quietly) literally rewires your brain

Meditators have always sworn by their practice. It is a hallmark practice in many Eastern religions and a supposed effective treatment for stress, anxiety, lack of focus, addictions, and more. But only recently have *scientists* discovered that the simple art of sitting down quietly with your thoughts can actually rewire the brain for the better. After just eleven hours of training, for example, neuroscientists have seen structural changes in novices (in brain regions critical for focus and self-control[3]).

Compared with people who don't meditate, meditators are great at policing their attention. With a little training and practice, you too can train your brain to stay on task longer, get distracted less easily, and overall operate more efficiently.

The simple act of bringing one's attention back to a point of focus, such as the breath (even if it's only for one or two breaths), has also been associated with:
- Increased willpower
- Enhanced functioning of the immune system
- Lower levels of stress chemicals such as cortisol (the molecule that makes you flip out whenever you have too much to do)
- Lengthening of telomeres—the little caps on your chromosomes which prevent aging
- An increase in grey matter (nerve cells)—more nerve tissue means a more connected and more efficient brain
- A decrease in size of the amygdala—essentially the "give a shit" center of your brain that causes fear and anxiety

The best and most popular meditation app is *Headspace*[4]. Sessions are ten minutes, guided, available on the go, and (best of all) free (various add-ons and themes are available for paying subscribers). UCLA's Free Guided Meditations[5] are excellent as well and include more variety.

If you aren't religious or still feel turned off by meditation for some reason, check out Tai Sheridan's *Buddha in Blue Jeans*[6]. It's short, available online for free, and suitable for people of all faiths.

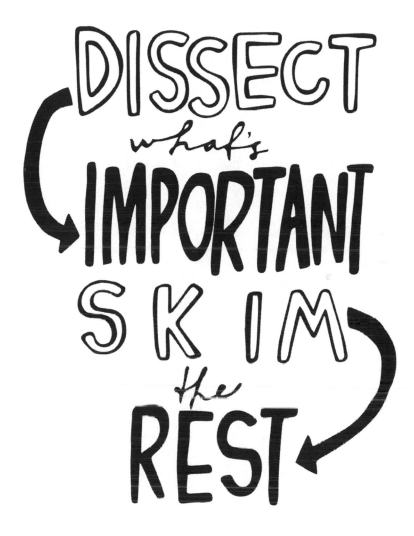

How to actually read better and faster (the ultimate superpower)

You already know how to read. I bet you were taught in grade school. But do you know how to read *well*? If you're like most people, you probably haven't given much thought to *how* you read. Yes, like any skill it can be improved!

In 2005, the world's two richest men, Bill Gates and Warren Buffett, sat down to talk to students at the University of Nebraska, Lincoln. When a student asked them what superpower they would want most, they both agreed on being able to read at lightning speed.

Here are the secrets of the best information consumers:
- The only way to become a better reader is to read. Many people have wasted a ton of money and time by failing to understand that last sentence.
- Always skim first. This engages the mind-wandering mode and helps you latch onto important ideas the second run-through.
- The best way to increase your speed is not to read everything. Determine what is important. Dissect and digest it. Then skim the rest.
- Know what you want before you read. Write down questions you want answered. Take notes on key points.
- Improve your fluency to increase your speed. Use Anki to learn new words and phrases.
- Read books that are beyond your level. Seek out the top authors. Reach.

To remember what you've just read, use retrieval. Read ten pages. Close the book. Write a one page or one paragraph summary. Don't just paraphrase, use your own words. Write down bullet points that you can apply elsewhere. People who follow this strategy remember mountains more than those try to internalize material by passively reading. It forces you to figure out the key points (and organize and process them). Plus, you'll have notes for later if you need a quick refresher.

For even more strategies, check out Mortimer Adler's classic *How to Read a Book*[7].

Underrated skills

Honestly rate your abilities in each of these areas (1 for awful, 10 for excellent).

Do you ask other people for help when you don't understand something?

Do you think about what you really need to learn before you start studying?

Do you create your own examples to make information more meaningful?

Do you focus on big-ticket concepts rather than specifics?

Do you ask yourself if what you're learning is related to what you already know?

Do you consider several possible ways of solving a problem before you answer?

Can you estimate how well you did once you finish a test?

Can you take a complex task and divide it into more manageable subtasks?

Can you prioritize when you are faced with multiple or complex tasks?

Can you choose feasible daily goals to accomplish?

How quickly can you start working on a task?

Can you stop during a task and check if you are on track?

Can you recognize when you are stressed or overwhelmed?

Can you stop and relax during stressful times?

How quickly do you notice mistakes?

How quickly can you address these mistakes?

Can you hold important information in mind in a distracting environment?

Can you ignore people, noise and other things going on around you, while working on a task?

Can you avoid making careless errors when doing a task?

Can you do a series of tasks in the most efficient order?

Can you follow a detailed plan and not get distracted?

How well can you manage your energy?

Can you recognize when you are too tired to perform well?

Can you set goals and achieve them in a reasonable amount of time?

Can you handle whatever comes your way without getting angry or frustrated?

Most people don't think of these areas as skills, but they're astoundingly important.

Sharpen them and you'll catch up to, and even overtake, the "naturally gifted."

Know yourself, and you'll achieve your goals.

Being able to control your behavior is a priceless gift.

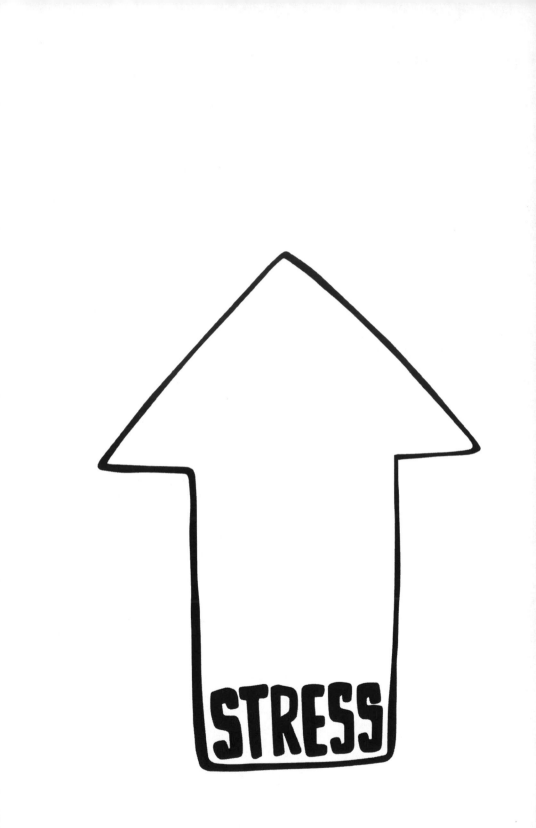

The upside of stress

Salvatore Maddi, who runs the Hardiness Research Lab at the University of California, Irvine, has dedicated his career to figuring out what distinguishes those who thrive under stress and those who are defeated by it. His conclusion: the best fighters know stress is inevitable. Rather than try to avoid it, they use high-pressure situations to adapt, learn and grow.

The idea that we can grow through adversity *isn't* new. The ability to learn from stress is built into our basic biology. The stress response produces DHEA and nerve growth factor, both of which increase neuroplasticity, or help your brain learn from experience. DHEA is a neurosteroid. In the same way that steroids make your muscles grow bigger from working out, DHEA helps your brain grow stronger from psychological setbacks (by remembering them and preparing you for next time).

We can predict whether a stressful situation will be strengthened by looking at hormones. Higher levels of cortisol, which suppresses the immune system, lead to undesirable outcomes like emotional instability and "analysis paralysis". On the contrary, higher levels of DHEA have been linked to reduced risk of anxiety, depression, heart problems and other diseases we typically think are caused by stress.

Psychologists call the ratio of DHEA to cortisol the *growth index*. This is what helps college students bounce back after failing a midterm, and prevents NAVY Seals from getting "stuck" when it matters most. This index is the holy grail—what you should aim to maximize—so you can thrive during and after stressful experiences.

Trying to avoid stress is fundamentally counterproductive. You will fail. But going through stress makes you better at handling it. It gets easier to face new challenges and deal with setbacks. An important question, then, is: how do I get better at stress?

Start thinking differently (notice a pattern?). Choose a more positive mindset toward stress. When you feel overwhelmed, make a conscious decision to view stress as helpful and the moment as an opportunity to improve your skills, knowledge, or strengths. This mental shift can actually tip the hormones in a useful direction, by increasing your growth index.

FALL IN

love

WITH READING

Fall in love with reading

"If I read a book that costs me $20 and I get one good idea, I've gotten one of the greatest bargains of all time."
- Tom Peters

In today's information age, there has never been a greater need to rapidly consume information and learn. Knowledge isn't just power anymore. It's profit. The rich, the successful, the impressive know this. They are all voracious readers. Steven Spielberg, Barack Obama, Stephen Colbert, Matt Damon, 50 Cent. Yes, all of them. LeBron James, too.

Do you know why? I have my guess. We all have one life to live. But when you read, you get to absorb the curated life of someone else—all the mistakes, all the successes, all the lessons. You get to relive history in a compact form, in days instead of decades.

With just a library card or a little money, you can download the consciousness of the wisest, smartest, healthiest, and most successful and impactful people in history. If you read a lot, your one brain can potentially hold on to the key lessons of thousands of other incredible people. You can bathe in their stories and come out a smarter you. You'll also improve your vocabulary and become a more skilled writer in the process. What an unbeatable deal!

Remember *Harlem Village Academies*? Every student in the fifth grade and up there reads fifty books a year. If the non-advantaged kids in one of the poorest, hardest neighborhoods in America can read fifty books a year, why can't every student? Why can't you?

The right book in the right hands at the right time can change the world. Now, keep reading!

Take ten (seconds)

After each class, talk, or significant experience, take ten seconds—no more, no less—to write down the most important point (MIP).

Just because you took perfect notes doesn't mean you're excused. This isn't note-taking. Though brief, this act is entirely different; it's an act of interpretation, prioritization, and elimination.

Avoid details, pierce through to the core idea. Jot the MIP quickly, otherwise you'll forget it in an hour or two.

Tell yourself each time, "I am taking away this lesson from this experience." This habit will help you learn to listen better and with more focus, ask more relevant questions, and accumulate actionable wisdom from everyone and everything. Although difficult and daunting at first, it gets easier with each practice round.

Go to class!

The importance of this rule cannot be overemphasized. It doesn't matter if your class meets at 8 a.m. on the far side of campus—wake up, get dressed, eat something, and show up to lecture on time. If you skip class, it'll likely take twice as much studying to make up for what you missed. This is why attendance is so critical: not because you're supposed to go, or because it's what your parents want, but because it saves time. Provided your professor's accent isn't so thick you can't understand him, if you attend class regularly and pay attention (at least a little), you'll drastically reduce the amount of studying you need to score high marks. Don't make this negotiable. Even if you're tired or drowning in work, find a way to make it there.

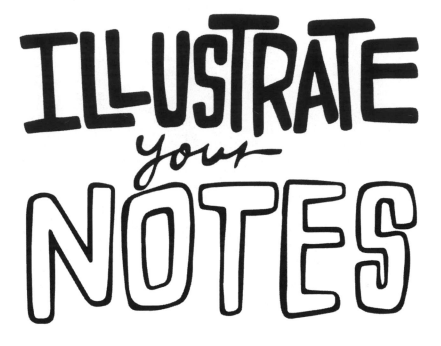

Top students don't take notes, they design them

"A lecture is a process by which the notes of the professor become the notes of the students without passing through the minds of either."
- R.K. Rathbun

Note-taking should be intuitive: pay attention, and scribble (or type) as the professor speaks and displays slides of information, right? Even though this is how most students take notes (by indiscriminately writing everything down in the same order it was presented), the answer is "no".

Luckily, Cal Newport, who runs the Web's most popular student advice blog (Study Hacks), has written multiple volumes on how to take notes. Here are his proven strategies:

For non-technical courses (basically anything that doesn't make frequent use of mathematical formulas):

The key to doing well: identify the big ideas (exams in these courses focus entirely on big ideas; explaining them, contrasting them, reevaluating them in light of new evidence).

Outline big ideas with the Question/Evidence/Conclusion structure. Your goal is to organize all the details and observations spewed out during class into this neat simple structure.

Don't attempt to record the lecture verbatim (you can still do a thorough job without capturing every little detail).

This is both impossible and counterproductive. You can't write that fast and will waste valuable energy capturing exact words, instead of big ideas.

Format your notes aggressively.

Date them. Use bold fonts and lists. Underline. Indent. Draw boxes or circles around ideas. Develop your own shorthand ("bc." for "because", "w." for "with", "NA" for "North America"). Skip lines. Change the font size. Use different colors. Write entire sentences in all caps. Have fun and do whatever helps you save time and visualize the big ideas. Your notes are for you and you alone; they don't need to make sense to anyone else.

Use lulls in the lecture (when the instructor goes on a tangent or a student asks an inane question) to hurriedly go back and clean up your notes if you're having trouble keeping up.

Review your notes right after class to absorb them and make any corrections or additions before you forget them.

For technical courses (any subject that makes heavy use of math or computer code):
- Record as many sample problems as possible.
- Make careful note of the steps taken and annotate them with little explanations of what they do or why they're important.
- Have your textbook or reading for the day open so you can refer to it if you get lost.

Note-taking is an art, and the first step in getting better at it is to recognize that not all the material presented is equally important. Get good at identifying and thinking hard about the important stuff, and you can ditch the rest.

Technology provides speed skates for learners

If all the teacher is going to do is read her pre-written bullet points from a PowerPoint slide to a classroom of twenty or a lecture hall of two hundred, perhaps she should stay home. Not only is this terribly disrespectful to the students, it's also complete waste of time. Teaching is no longer about delivering facts that can be found elsewhere in another format. Teachers need to be great, or they'll be replaced (by the Internet).

Khan Academy, for example, offers thousands of online videos that (for free) teach everything from art to world history to calculus. To date, the lectures have been delivered hundreds of millions of times. Founder Sal Khan's goal for the future: to create a free, universal library of courses online, accessible to anyone in the world with an Internet connection. Lectures on every conceivable topic, constantly improved. This means that every student will be able to watch precisely the lecture she needs, at her own speed, as many times as she wants.

In 2001, the Massachusetts Institute of Technology put all of its courses online. Imagine that: the finest technical university in the world sharing every course it offers with any student who is willing to expend the effort to learn.

Stanford and hundreds of other prestigious universities have followed suit, using their materials to create free online classes on platforms such as *edX, Coursera*, and *Udacity*. What's even more amazing: some of these courses have over 100,000 active students at any given time.

It gets better. Google is scanning millions of book titles a year. With *YouTube EDU* and *iTunesU*, you can view video and audio lectures from the best professors in the world, as well as materials from museums and cultural institutions, all for free. Entrepreneurs are even creating online programs to act as sophisticated tutors. They're like teachers, but with infinite patience, undivided attention, and an unlimited number of examples and hints. Awesome, right?

What else? *Wikipedia* (need I say more). *Slader* (every math problem in hundreds of editions of dozens of math textbooks, solved). *Quora* (a question-and-answer site where you can ask tons of smart people anything you want). *Griti* (a new website that connects students to step-by-step video walkthroughs custom-made for their exact college courses, taught by experts who got A's).

In *DIY U*, Anya Kamenetz writes: "Parents, peers, and teachers may be helpful or supportive, or they may stand in your way. No matter where you find yourself, the key is realizing you have more options for shaping your own education than almost anyone has ever had at this point in history." She's right. The resources keep growing and improving. You can make school what you need it to be *for you*. The future is bright.

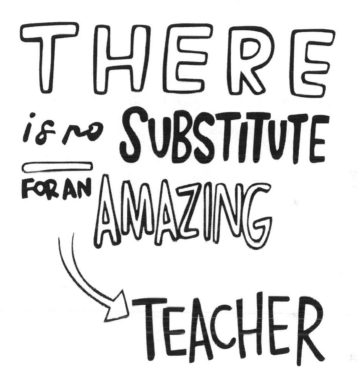

There is no substitute for an amazing teacher

Truly great teachers:
- Know their subject matter extremely well
- Prepare for teaching sessions as serious intellectual endeavours
- Make the material seem both simple and profound
- Don't just pile on assignments
- Avoid judging students on arbitrary standards (they focus more on growth over time)
- Have a good idea of what mental models students are likely to bring with them into class and which ones they need to challenge
- Realize where people are likely to have difficulties developing their own comprehension
- Make an effort to teach students what they want to learn about
- Set up systems to help students learn from each other
- Test for understanding
- CARE

When you get the chance to interact with a talented educator or mentor like this, seize it. Force yourself to reach out and ask questions—real, specific, important questions, not questions meant to show off what you know or to get the teacher to like you. A simple sentence or piece of advice from their vast set of life experiences can change the course of your future.

If none of your teachers match this description, your go-to solution should be a different teacher, a friend or the Internet. There are so many options nowadays.

CHAPTER
MOVING FORWARD

The media will always get science wrong

People went crazy about Mozart in the 1990s. They proclaimed that his music could improve test-taking ability. That it could heal the body. That it could make babies smarter. In 1998, Zell Miller, the then governor of Georgia, even announced that he wanted the state to spend $105,000 a year to provide every child born in Georgia with a tape or CD of classical music. Yet the "Mozart effect", as it was called, proved to be garbage. More than twenty follow-up experiments failed to reproduce the results of the original (and poorly designed) study[1]. The trumpets were for nothing.

Every day, we see another provocative article on Facebook about the latest breakthrough study. Does Advil cause dementia? Can video games cure ADHD? Will Luminosity make you smarter? Is driving dehydrated the same as driving drunk?

This shouldn't be a surprise. Media outlets need to grab attention fast and leave their readers with a key takeaway. Words and space are limited. Competition is fierce.

Most people would rather be punched in the face multiple times than be forced to carefully read "Association of dietary, circulating, and supplement fatty acids with coronary risk: a systematic review and meta-analysis." That's why the New York Times article that covered the key nutritional paper was simply "Butter is Back"[2].

Unfortunately, I have a sad truth for you. Science is imperfect and usually boring. Shocking discoveries made by lone geniuses don't happen anymore. The field advances slowly; researchers are wrong all the time. It takes years for anything useful to be found. Funding is scarce. *Most research isn't deserving of a headline—or even close.*

In an effort to illustrate how often medical studies can be flawed, the popular news website *Vox* put together a graph showing how common foods like coffee, beef, and butter are linked to cancer[3]. Their conclusion: everything we eat both causes and prevents cancer, because you can get some very different results based on how you design your experiment (which is based heavily on who puts up the money for the study—usually large corporations with interests to protect).

Still not convinced most science journalists pawn off untrue or incomplete information as fact? *Time* once ran the headline "Scientists Say Smelling Farts Might Prevent Cancer"[4]. The study mentioned[5], however, never talked about "farts", or "cancer". Fortunately, reader backlash prompted Time to change the headline and issue this correction three days later: "An earlier version of this article incorrectly summarized the findings and implications of this study." In other words, the journalist fibbed everything to drive clicks.

Society will always be attracted to the flashy headline. Marketers will try to tell us that one thing or activity or product can make you smarter. More productive. More successful. Happier. A better person. Don't get suckered into this "get something for nothing" mentality. It's an overly simplistic approach.

No, Adderall will not make you go blind. No, using a laptop in class will not lower your chances of getting an A. And no, Jersey Shore will not lower your IQ (even though I have some doubts about this).

The point is: catchy titles aren't going away, so be critical. Ask questions. Look at the source. See if the findings actually apply to *you*. Consult with experts. Default to skepticism.

Real geniuses work hard

"It takes twenty years to become an overnight success."
- Eddie Cantor

The smartest, most successful, most impactful people in the world—who everyone writes stories about—don't succeed because of their genes. They make it to the top because they work the hardest and are the most determined[6]. Plain and simple. They master the art of learning and follow a simple but disciplined strategy. They are always feeding their curiosity. They are constantly growing. They are in it for the long haul. They know that perseverance is a great substitute for talent.

Don't listen to the people who tell you that smart people get things immediately. Don't listen to the people who tell you that successful people never fail or never make mistakes. Don't listen to the people who tell you that you'll never get there. These people are liars. Start wherever you are. Progress as fast as you can. Celebrate the small victories along the way. Involve other people. Reflect.

You can't teach yourself world history over the weekend or expect to be the best mathematician in the world, but you can be patient and persistent. You can make the most out of the opportunities you are given. Like a baby, you can start with learning how to crawl, and then how to walk (and then maybe even how to run). If it's really not working out, then of course move on. But don't give up so damn early. Learning takes time.

There will always be the blamers. They blame their textbook, or their teachers, or their genetics. You're not going to be a blamer. You are going to be someone who says it can be learned, and then does it.

The way I see it, there are only two paths you can take:

Option 1

Believe intelligence is static and abilities are fixed. Desire to look smart. Avoid challenges. Give up easily. Ignore criticism. Be threatened by the success of others. Plateau early. Achieve less than your full potential. Feel out of control.

Option 2

Have faith that you can become smarter and understand better. Learn and read and teach. Embrace struggle. Learn from failure. Be persistent. See effort and experimentation as the path to mastery. Accept and act on criticism. Find lessons and inspiration in the success of others. Get advice from those who are more knowledgeable and more experienced than you. Make small steps forward. Reach ever-higher levels of achievements. Feel in control.

No one is born great, but everyone is born with the ability to become great. So, which option do you pick? How do you want to be viewed by others? Who do you want to surround yourself with? What do you want your future to look like? The choice is yours.

EXPERIMENT

Advance through trial and error

"Whatever we learn to do, we learn by actually doing it; men come to be builders, for instance, by building, and harp players by playing the harp."
- Aristotle

No matter how much you love or hate this book, you're unlikely to be an expert learner. The marketing for this book likely promised you'd be a better student for reading it. I think that's true on one condition: you practice. But I know most people are lazy. I can be lazy.

Don't be lazy.

There will always be a shortage of good learners in the world, no matter how many good books on the subject. It's a performance skill, like drawing or public speaking or running the hundred-meter dash, and performance means practice.

Again, reading this book is great—I thank you—but it's not enough. With a subject like learning, exposing yourself to "best practices" does not suffice—it's just intellectual tourism. You need to play with the material. Test it. Teach it. See what works for you, and replace what doesn't. Determine if the experts are actually right—who knows, you might find out something they don't know.

One of my favorite definitions of insanity is doing something over and over again and expecting a different result. So pick a strong strategy, and adjust as you go. Don't be afraid to mix things up. Your results *will* improve over time.

FORGET ABOUT FORMAL EDUCATION

Forget about formal education

"I have never let my schooling interfere with my education."
- Mark Twain

You don't need a degree from an Ivy League university to be successful. You don't need to study twenty hours a day to get a perfect GPA or get admitted to a top graduate program. And you sure as hell don't need to major in science, technology, engineering, or math (STEM) to get a good job.

I know this all sounds obvious when you *really* think about it, but many people forget there are a million ways to make it in this world. To learn. To find a mentor. To be influential. To make money. To get to the next level. To get the life you want.

Many of the world's biggest and best companies—Facebook, Apple, Microsoft, Dell, Ford, Ralph Lauren—were started by people who dropped out of college or didn't go in the first place. Richard Branson, the founder of Virgin, didn't even finish high school.

Most Fortune 500 CEOs didn't go to Harvard or Stanford, or any prestigious university for that matter.

Let me repeat: you don't need a piece of paper or permission from some bureaucrat to get an education, or to be valuable in society.

Additionally, no matter what you think, a university degree is not a passport to easy success. Two to three years out of college, no one will care where you went. It'll be about what you know and what you've done. How quickly you can learn new topics (otherwise, you'll fall behind) and how well you can solve problems. How you handle failure and adversity.

So, if you feel you don't have the educational advantages others do, don't worry. Most people don't. But access to information isn't the issue. You have books, museums, radio, podcasts, smart people in your neighborhood, and the Internet (my God, what a gift!). Don't wait for some institution or someone to pick you. Pick yourself. Teach yourself. Motivate yourself. Your responsibility is to make the best use of whatever resources come your way. What are you waiting for?

Learning doesn't stop after you graduate

"There is no end to education. It is not that you read a book, pass an examination, and finish with education. The whole of life, from the moment you are born to the moment you die, is a process of learning."
- Jiddu Krishnamurti

Class gets out in five minutes. Eyes light up. Backpacks start to zip. Attention is long gone.

The bells rings. It's a race to the hall, to freedom. Not a single student sticks around.

This happens, five or six times a day, in every classroom, every day of the school year. Then graduation rolls around. "How great! No one is forcing me to learn things I don't want to learn anymore!" students exclaim. But with no more grades to serve as motivation, curiosity dies. In the "real world", there is no test, and there is no teacher. Growth halts. People get stuck and unhappy. Eventually they settle.

It's in our nature to *need* a plan. To seek control. To appear stable and to appear competent (especially to others). But that won't get you anywhere. Life moves fast, institutions topple, wars start, industries die, movements begin, technology advances. People, including you, change. Your plans will shatter. Your forecasts will never materialize. Your predictions will be wrong.

A smart person knows this. He embraces it. He lives it. He makes an educated guess and then puts his foot on the gas pedal, adjusting as he goes. Unlike the planners, unlike the forecasters, unlike the doubters and the excuse-makers, he experiments. He fails, but he learns. Continually. He accumulates mistakes, and then never lets them happen again. He reads. He acquires wisdom from others. He puts his head down and *keeps moving forward*.

No one has it figured it out. No one ever will. No one. A master knows he will change course every so often and that's OK. A master knows he will never "arrive".

A degree isn't enough to keep you going for forty years. Much of what you learn in school will be outdated or irrelevant a few years after you get out anyways; the pace of progress is too fast.

Class is never dismissed. Don't be frozen in time. Desire lifelong learning, integrate it with life, and you will get and stay ahead.

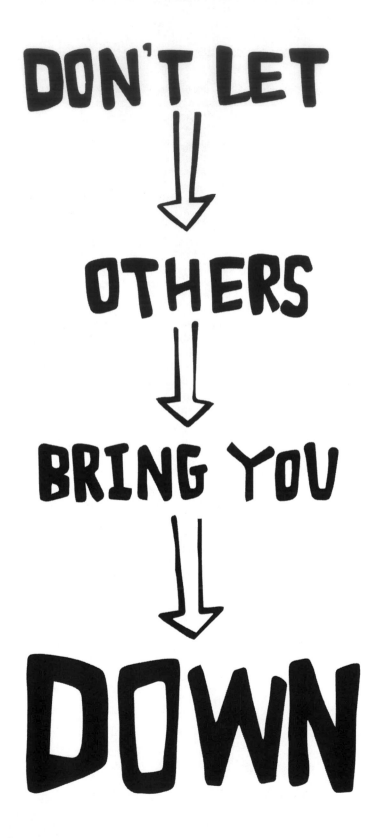

There will always be intellectual critics

There will always be those people who undermine any effort or achievement you make. If you do well in your studies, they will feel threatened, become jealous, and try to diminish your success. On the flip side, if you flunk a test, there will be those who say you don't have what it takes. They will try to position themselves above you and make you feel inadequate.

Your default response in either case should be not to give them the light of day. Failure is informative. Analyze what you did wrong and make sure you adjust for the future. If you find yourself struggling with what others think is "obvious", don't despair. Look to friends or the Internet for help. Find people who have been in your position and ask them to share their experiences with you.

As you will find when you reach the real world (if you haven't already), people are far more interested in making themselves look good and furthering their own objectives than helping you. Keep yourself open to constructive criticism, but recognize when criticism that is masked as helpful is really just hurtful.

Take pride in who you are, especially in your strengths and what makes you unique, and use them as a secret talisman for success. Indulge your curiosity as often as possible, dive into your interests with fervor, and don't let anyone tell you "no". Now go forth, learn, and triumph.

CHAPTER
REVIEW

Key learning principles

- Use recall to see whether you can actually reproduce something from memory
- Test yourself as early as possible
- Chunk up concepts
- Space your repetition
- Interleave (mix it up)
- Talk things out
- Do the hard problems first, then jump to the easy ones
- Attention is a limited-capacity resource
- Distractions are deadly
- Vary your learning environments
- Involve as many senses as possible (especially vision)
- Make use of mental contrasting
- You learn while you sleep
- Read good books that interest you
- Learn at least a little bit every day

10 commandments of studying

1. Learn the fundamentals first
2. Don't move on until you learn the fundamentals
3. Focus intensely when it's time to study
4. Work in short bursts to keep your energy levels high
5. Take breathers or meditate to help clear mental barriers
6. Always skim first and don't read everything
7. Exercise regularly
8. Drink lots of water and keep healthy snacks handy
9. Ask questions and clear up points of confusion immediately
10. Get feedback from those more knowledgeable and more experienced than you

Avoid like the plague

- Rereading
- Highlighting/underlining everything
- Simply glancing at a problem's solution and telling yourself you know how to do it
- Cramming
- Overlearning (doing problems you know how to do over and over again)
- Letting study sessions turn into chat sessions
- Multitasking
- Too much sugar or caffeine
- All-nighters

CHAPTER
NOTES

First
1. McNamara, D. S. (2000). "Preliminary Analysis of Photoreading." Prepared for NASA Ames Research Center. Grant Number: NAG-2-1319.
    ntrs.nasa.gov/archive/nasa/casi.ntrs.nasa.gov/20000011599.pdf

Myths
1. Gardner, H., & Hatch, T. (1989). "Multiple Intelligences Go to School: Educational Implications of the Theory of Multiple Intelligences". *Educational Researcher 18(8)*: 4-10.
    www.sfu.ca/~jcnesbit/EDUC220/ThinkPaper/Gardner1989.pdf
2. There are two main types of intelligence scientists like to talk about. The first is called crystallized intelligence, or *what you know*. The other is fluid intelligence, *how you think*. IQ tests are primarily tests of crystallized intelligence. They reward people who *know* more, who paid attention and learned more, not the intrinsically more talented. This is precisely why IQ scores drop over summer and then rise again in the fall when students go back to school.
3. www.beginwiththebrain.com/resources/8_kinds_of_smart.pdf
4. Bloom, B. S. (1984). "The 2 Sigma Problem: The Search for Methods of Group Instruction as Effective as One-on-One Tutoring." *Educational Researcher 13(6)*: 4-16.
    web.mit.edu/5.95/readings/bloom-two-sigma.pdf
5. Robynne Boyd, "Do People Only Use 10 Percent of Their Brains?" *Scientific American*, February 7, 2008.
    www.scientificamerican.com/article/do-people-only-use-10-percent-of-their-brains
6. Pashler, H. (2008). "Learning Styles: Concepts and Evidence." *Psychological Science in the Public Interest 9(3)*: 105-119.
    www.psychologicalscience.org/journals/pspi/PSPI_9_3.pdf?utm_source=hootsuite
7. This may not apply to those with legitimate learning disabilities, such as dyslexia.
8. Nielsen J. A., et al. (2013). "An Evaluation of the Left-Brain vs. Right-Brain Hypothesis with Resting State Functional Connectivity Magnetic Resonance Imaging." *PLoS ONE 8(8)*:
    e71275. dx.doi.org/10.1371/journal.pone.0071275
9. www.reddit.com/r/IAmA/comments/2rgsan/i_am_elon_musk_ceocto_of_a_rocket_company_ama

Neuroplasticity
1. Every cab driver in central London has to have "The Knowledge"—a memorized map, including 25,000 streets and thousands of tourist attractions and hot spots. It's a brutal learning process that can take three to four years to complete, with a final test that often take a dozen attempts to pass. Even then, only about 40% of hopeful pass. In 2000, English neuroscientist Eleanor Maguire discovered that learning this mental atlas of England's capital causes structural changes to the brain. Compared to people of similar age, education and intelligence, these taxi drivers had more neurons and greater connectivity in the *hippocampus*, a region of the brain important for long-term memory and navigation. The longer the cabbie had been driving, the more pronounced the effect. The old wisdom of the brain being fixed is simply not true.

    Maguire, E. A. (2006). "London Taxi Drivers and Bus Drivers: A Structural MRI and Neuropsychological Analysis." *Hippocampus 16*.
    cvcl.mit.edu/SUNSeminar/MaguireWolletSpiers06Hippocampus.pdf
2. Sadly, orphans and neglected children often have low IQs, delayed language skills, and other learning difficulties. The reason: developing brains that are not given the proper, "expected" environment—one that involves novelty, challenge, exercise, proper nutrition, and love—struggle to develop normally. Encouragingly, once these children are removed to a safe, loving environment, their brains are able to recover (to varying

degrees). The earlier the intervention, the better.
3. Contrary to popular belief, if you just show up and work hard (and that's it), you'll soon hit a performance plateau—because the amount of myelin around your circuits won't be changing.

Attention
1. Flow, the secret to happiness. Mihaly Csikszentmihalyi (2004). www.ted.com/talks/mihaly_csikszentmihalyi_on_flow?language=en
2. youtu.be/IGQmdoK_ZfY
3. www.theoryofknowledge.info/theories-of-perception/naive-realism

Memory
1. MRI scans of these mental athletes indeed show that their brains are no different structurally from the rest of ours. Their IQs aren't anything special either.
2. www.skillstoolbox.com/career-and-education-skills/learning-skills/memory-skills/mnemonics/mnemonic-systems/loci-mnemonic-system

Studying
1. Pashler, H., et al. (2008). "Spacing effects learning: A temporal ridgeline of optimal retention." *Psychological Science 19(11)*: 1095-1102. wixtedlab.ucsd.edu/publications/wixted/Cepeda_Vul_Rohrer_Wixted_Pashler.pdf
2. ankisrs.net
3. rs.io/anki-tips
4. leitnerportal.com/LearnMore.aspx
5. Rittle-Johnson, B., et al. (2007). "Learning from explaining: does it matter if mom is listening?" *Journal of Experimental Child Psychology 100(3)*: 215-224.

Testing
1. An effective way to avoid falling for wrong answers on multiple choice tests is to immediately cover the answers and attempt to recall the answer from memory. Choosing a solution this way will prevent you from picking an answer too quickly or simply picking an answer because it makes some sense at the time.
2. Richard Felder, "Memo to Students Who Have Been Disappointed with Their Test Grades." *Chemical Engineering Education*, 33(2), 136-37 (1999). www4.ncsu.edu/unity/lockers/users/f/felder/public/Columns/memo.pdf

Problem Solving
1. Merim Bilali and Peter McLeod, "Why Your First Idea Can Blind You to a Better One." *Scientific American*, March 1, 2014. www.scientificamerican.com/article/why-your-first-idea-can-blind-you-to-better-idea

Creativity
1. Zeigarnik, B. (1927). "On Finished and Unfinished Tasks." *Psychologische Forschung 9*. www.codeblab.com/wp-content/uploads/2009/12/On-Finished-and-Unfinished-Tasks.pdf
2. Uzzi, B., et al. (2011). "Atypical Combinations and Scientific Impact." *Science 342*: 468-472. www.kellogg.northwestern.edu/faculty/uzzi/htm/papers/science-2013-uzzi-468-72.pdf

Productivity
1. Gailliot, M. T., Baumeister, R. F., et al. (2007). "Self-Control Relies on Glucose as a

Limited Energy Source: Willpower Is More Than a Metaphor." *Journal of Personality and Social Psychology 92(2)*. 325-336.
www.uky.edu/~njdewa2/gailliotetal07JPSP.pdf
2. www.chrome.google.com/webstore/detail/strict-workflow/cgmnfnmlficgeijcalkgnnkigkefkbhd?hl=en
3. Susie Cranston and Steve Keller, "Increasing the 'meaning quotient' of work." *McKinsey Quarterly*, January 2013.
www.mckinsey.com/business-functions/organization/our-insights/increasing-the-meaning-quotient-of-work
4. www.flowgenomeproject.com/flow-fundamentals

Sleep
1. Maria Popova, "Thomas Edison, Power- Napper: The Great Inventor on Sleep and Success." *Brain Pickings*, February 11, 2013.
www.brainpickings.org/2013/02/11/thomas-edison-on-sleep-and-success
2. justgetflux.com

Languages
1. You can easily find premade decks of the most frequently used words in a language (or words themed around a subject you might want to talk about) online.
2. www.fluentin3months.com/free-links
3. Catherine de Lange, "Age no excuse for failing to learn a new language." *New Scientist*, July 20, 2011.
www.newscientist.com/article/mg21128224.000-age-no-excuse-for-failing-to-learn-a-new-language
4. www.chrome.google.com/webstore/detail/language-immersion-for-ch/bedbecnakfcpmkpddjfnfihogkaggkhl/related
5. Vesselinov, R., & Grego, J. (2012). "Duolingo Effectiveness Study." Final Report, manuscript available through Duolingo.
www.static.duolingo.com/s3/DuolingoReport_Final.pdf
6. www.fourhourworkweek.com/podcast

Tips, Tricks, and Hacks
1. Bramble, D. M., & Lieberman, D. E. (2007). "The Evolution of Marathon Running." *Sports Med 37(4-5)*: 288-290.
www.fas.harvard.edu/~skeleton/pdfs/2007c.pdf
2. www.amazon.com/Spark-Revolutionary-Science-Exercise-Brain/dp/0316113514
3. Tang Y., Lu Q., Geng X., Stein E. A., Yang Y., & Posner M. I. (2010). "Short term mental training induces white-matter changes in the anterior cingulate." *PNAS 104(43)*: 17152-56.
www.ncbi.nlm.nih.gov/pmc/articles/PMC2040428/pdf/zpq17152.pdf
4. www.headspace.com
5. marc.ucla.edu/body.cfm?id=22
6. www.holybooks.com/wp-content/uploads/Buddha-in-Blue-Jean.pdf
7. www.evergladeshs.org/ourpages/auto/2015/5/28/58122395/Adler%20Mortimer%20-%20How%20To%20Read%20A%20Book.pdf

Moving Forward
1. Rauscher, F. H., Shaw, G. L. & Ky, K. N. (1993). "Music and Spatial Task Performance: A Causal Relationship." *Nature*, 365, 611.
files.eric.ed.gov/fulltext/ED390733.pdf
2. Mark Bittman, "Butter is Back." *New York Times: The Opinion Pages*, March 25, 2014.
www.nytimes.com/2014/03/26/opinion/bittman-butter-is-back.html

3. Bec Crew, "Everything We Eat Both Causes and Prevents Cancer." *ScienceAlert*, April 1, 2015.
    www.sciencealert.com/everything-we-eat-both-causes-and-prevents-cancer
4. Laura Stampler, "A Stinky Compound May Protect Against Cell Damage, Study Finds." *Time*, July 11, 2014.
    www.time.com/2976464/rotten-eggs-hydrogen-sulfide-mitochondria/
5. Szczesny B., Módis K., Yanagi K., Coletta C., et al. (2014). "AP39, a novel mitochondria-targeted hydrogen sulfide donor, stimulates cellular bioenergetics, exerts cytoprotective effects and protects against the loss of mitochondrial DNA integrity in oxidatively stressed endothelial cells in vitro." *Nitric Oxide, 41*, 120-130.
6. Sometimes, you can work the hardest and be the most determined but be in the wrong place at the wrong time, and receive little praise for your work. In many cases, successful people must also have a bit of luck—be in the right place at the right time. Look into Outliers by Malcolm Gladwell for a different perspective on success.

CHAPTER
RESOURCES

Worthwhile articles

Benedict Carey, "Cognitive science meets pre-algebra." *New York Times*, September 2, 2013.
www.nytimes.com/2013/09/03/science/cognitive-science-meets-pre-algebra.html?page
wanted=all

Christopher Wanjek, "Left Brain vs. Right: It's a Myth, Research Finds." *Live Science*, September 3, 2013.
www.livescience.com/39373-left-brain-right-brain-myth.html

Daniel J. Levitin, "Hit the Reset Button in Your Brain." *The New York Times*, August 9, 2014.
www.nytimes.com/2014/08/10/opinion/sunday/hit-the-reset-button-in-your-brain.html

Ferris Jabr, "Why Walking Helps Us Think." *The New Yorker*, September 3, 2014.
www.newyorker.com/tech/elements/walking-helps-us-think

James Morehead, "Stanford University's Carol Dweck on the Growth Mindset and Education." *OneDublin.org*, June 19, 2012.
www.onedublin.org/2012/06/19/stanford-universitys-carol-dweck-on-the-growth-
mindset-and-education

Jay Mathews, "Self-Discipline May Beat Smarts as Key to Success." *The Washington Post*, January 17, 2006.
www.washingtonpost.com/wp-dyn/content/article/2006/01/16/AR2006011600788.html

Joanna Penn, "The pen is mightier than the keyboard: Advantages of longhand over laptop note taking." *Journalist's Resource*, July 30, 2014.
journalistsresource.org/studies/society/education/longhand-versus-laptop-note-taking

John Hamilton, "Brains Sweep Themselves Clean of Toxins During Sleep." *NPR All Things Considered*, October 17, 2013.
www.npr.org/sections/health-shots/2013/10/18/236211811/brains-sweep-themselves-
clean-of-toxins-during-sleep

Johns Hopkins Medicine, "Memories of errors foster faster learning." *Science Daily*, August 14, 2014.
www.sciencedaily.com/releases/2014/08/140814191352.htm

Julia Belluz, "This is why you shouldn't believe that exciting new medical study." *Vox*, August 5, 2015.
www.vox.com/2015/3/23/8264355/research-study-hyp

Lauren Davidson, "This Is the Kind of Music You Should Listen to at Work." *The Telegraph*, October 23, 2014.
www.telegraph.co.uk/finance/newsbysector/mediatechnologyandtelecoms/11179017/
This-is-the-kind-of-music-you-should-listen-to-at-work.html

Michael Friedman, "Note-taking tools and tips." *Harvard Initiative for Learning and Teaching*, October 15, 2014.
hilt.harvard.edu/blog/note-taking-tools-and-tips

Pam Belluck, "To Really Learn, Quit Studying and Take a Test." *The New York Times*, January 20,

2011.
www.nytimes.com/2011/01/21/science/21memory.html

Robyn Scott, "The 30 Second Habit That Can Have a Big Impact On Your Life." *The Huffington Post*, February 18, 2014.
www.huffingtonpost.com/robyn-scott/the-30-second-habit-that-_b_4808632.html

Scott Young, "I was wrong about speed reading: Here are the facts." January 2015.
www.scotthyoung.com/blog/2015/01/19/speed-reading-redo

Travis Bradberry, "Multitasking Damages Your Brain And Career, New Studies Suggest." *Forbes*, October 8, 2014.
www.forbes.com/sites/travisbradberry/2014/10/08/multitasking-damages-your-brain-and-career-new-studies-suggest/#61c253e32c16

Popular talks

A simple way to break a bad habit. Judson Brewer (2015).
www.ted.com/talks/judson_brewer_a_simple_way_to_break_a_bad_habit

Changing education paradigms. Sir Ken Robinson (2010).
www.youtube.com/watch?v=zDZFcDGpL4U&list=PL39BF9545D740ECFF&index=9

Don't eat the marshmallow! Joachim de Posada (2009).
www.ted.com/talks/joachim_de_posada_says_don_t_eat_the_marshmallow_yet?language=en

Do schools kill creativity? Sir Ken Robinson (2006).
www.ted.com/talks/ken_robinson_says_schools_kill_creativity

Flow, the secret to happiness. Mihaly Csikszentmihalyi (2004).
www.ted.com/talks/mihaly_csikszentmihalyi_on_flow?language=en

How brain science will change computing. Jeff Hawkins (2003).
www.ted.com/talks/jeff_hawkins_on_how_brain_science_will_change_computing?language=en

How games make kids smarter. Gabe Zichermann (2011).
www.ted.com/talks/gabe_zichermann_how_games_make_kids_smarter

How to help every child fulfill their potential. Carol Dweck (2015).
www.youtube.com/watch?v=YI9TVbAaI5s&list=PL39BF9545D740ECFF&index=1

Growing evidence of brain plasticity. Michael Merzenich (2005).
www.ted.com/talks/michael_merzenich_on_the_elastic_brain?language=en

Kids can teach themselves. Sugata Mitra (2007).
www.ted.com/talks/sugata_mitra_shows_how_kids_teach_themselves?language=en

Let's use video to reinvent education. Salman Khan (2011).
www.ted.com/talks/salman_khan_let_s_use_video_to_reinvent_education?language=en

One more reason to get a good night's sleep. Jeff Iliff (2014).
www.ted.com/talks/jeff_iliff_one_more_reason_to_get_a_good_night_s_sleep

Smash fear, learn anything. Timothy Ferriss (2008).
www.ted.com/talks/tim_ferriss_smash_fear_learn_anything?language=en#t-808507

The divided brain and the making of the Western world. Iain McGilchrist (2011).
www.youtube.com/watch?v=dFs9WO2B8uI&list=PL39BF9545D740ECFF&index=6

The first 20 hours - how to learn anything. Josh Kaufman (2013).
www.youtube.com/watch?v=5MgBikgcWnY

What we're learning from online education. Daphne Koller (2012).
www.ted.com/talks/daphne_koller_what_we_re_learning_from_online_education

Why eyewitnesses get it wrong. Scott Fraser (2012).
www.ted.com/talks/scott_fraser_the_problem_with_eyewitness_testimony

You can grow new brain cells, here's how. Sandrine Thuret (2015).
www.ted.com/talks/sandrine_thuret_you_can_grow_new_brain_cells_here_s_how?language=en

Your brain on video games. Daphne Bavelier (2012).
www.ted.com/talks/daphne_bavelier_your_brain_on_video_games?language=en

Your elusive creative genius. Elizabeth Gilbert (2009).
www.ted.com/talks/elizabeth_gilbert_on_genius

Influential papers

Baumeister, R. F., et al. (1998). "Ego Depletion: Is the Active Self a Limited Resource?" *Journal of Personality and Social Psychology 74(5)*: 1252-65.
faculty.washington.edu/jdb/345/345%20Articles/Baumeister%20et%20al.%20(1998).pdf

Bilalić, M., et al. (2008). "Does chess need intelligence?—A study with young chess players." *Intelligence 35(5)*: 457-470.
www.sciencedirect.com/science/article/pii/S0160289606001139

Bilalić, M., et al. (2008). "Why good thoughts block better ones: The mechanism of the pernicious Einstellung (set) effect." *Cognition 108(3)*: 652-661.
chessmaine.net/chessmaine/EinstellungEffect.pdf

Bjork, R. A., et al. (2003). "Self-regulated learning: Beliefs, techniques, and illusions." *Annual Review of Psychology 64*: 417-444.
www.annualreviews.org/doi/pdf/10.1146/annurev-psych-113011-143823

Cowan, N. (2001). "The magical number 4 in short-term memory: A reconsideration of mental storage capacity." *Behavioral and Brain Sciences*, 24(1): 87-114.
journals.cambridge.org/download.php?file=%2FBBS%2FBBS24_01%2FS0140525X01003922a.pdf&code=ada981a3b80a82e32cf84720c13bb8d5

Csikszentmihalyi, M., & LaFevre, J. (1989). "Optimal experience in work and leisure." *Journal of Personality and Social Psychology 56(5)*. 815-822.
citeseerx.ist.psu.edu/viewdoc/download?doi=10.1.1.471.1586&rep=rep1&type=pdf

Dunlosky, J., et al. (2013). "Improving students' learning with effective learning techniques: Promising directions from cognitive and educational psychology." *Psychological Science in the Public Interest 14(1)*: 4-58.
www.indiana.edu/~pcl/rgoldsto/courses/dunloskyimprovinglearning.pdf

Ellenbogen, J. M., et al. (2007). "Human Relational Memory Requires Time and Sleep." *Proceedings of the National Academy of Sciences*, 104(18): 7723-28.
www.researchgate.net/profile/Jessica_Payne/publication/6378577_Human_relational_memory_requires_time_and_sleep/links/0912f500ecdcb765cf000000.pdf

Ericsson, K. A., et al. (1993). "The role of deliberate practice in the acquisition of expert performance." *Psychological Review 100(3)*: 363-406.
projects.ict.usc.edu/itw/gel/EricssonDeliberatePracticePR93.pdf

Fields, R. D. (2015). "A new mechanism of nervous system plasticity: activity-dependent myelination." *Nature Reviews Neuroscience 16(12)*: 756-767.
www.nature.com/nrn/journal/v16/n12/pdf/nrn4023.pdf

Kornell, N., et al. (2009). "Unsuccessful retrieval attempts enhance subsequent learning" *Journal of Experimental Psychology: Learning, Memory, and Cognition 35(4)*: 210-216.
sites.williams.edu/nk2/files/2011/08/Kornell.Hays_.Bjork_.2009.pdf

Maguire, E., et al. (2003). "Routes to remembering: the brains behind superior memory." *Nature Neuroscience 6(1)*: 90-95.
www.nature.com/neuro/journal/v6/n1/pdf/nn988.pdf

Mueller, A., et al. (2008). "Sleep deprivation can inhibit adult hippocampal neurogenesis independent of adrenal stress hormones." *American Journal of Physiology - Regulatory, Integrative and Comparative Physiology 294(5)*: 1693-1703.
ajpregu.physiology.org/content/ajpregu/294/5/R1693.full.pdf

Pashler, H., et al. (2008). "Spacing effects learning: A temporal ridgeline of optimal retention." *Psychological Science 19(11)*. 1095-1102.
wixtedlab.ucsd.edu/publications/wixted/Cepeda_Vul_Rohrer_Wixted_Pashler.pdf

Pashler, H., et al. (2009). "Learning Styles: Concepts and Evidence." *Psychological Science in the Public Interest 9(3)*: 106-118.
www.psychologicalscience.org/journals/pspi/PSPI_9_3.pdf?utm_source=hootsuite

Roediger, H. L., & Karpicke, J. D. (2006). "Test-Enhanced Learning Taking Memory Tests Improves Long-Term Retention." *Association for Psychological Science 17(3)*: 249-255.
learninglab.psych.purdue.edu/downloads/2006_Roediger_Karpicke_PsychSci.pdf

Roediger, H. L., & Butler, A. C. (2011). "The critical role of retrieval practice in long-term retention." *Trends in Cognitive Sciences 15(1)*: 20-27.
www.cell.com/trends/cognitive-sciences/pdf/S1364-6613(10)00208-1.pdf

Rohrer, D., & Pashler, H. (2007). "Increasing retention without increasing study time. *Current Directions in Psychological Science 16(4)*: 183-86.
www.pashler.com/Articles/RohrerPashler2007CDPS.pdf

Sana, F., et al. (2013). "Laptop multitasking hinders classroom learning for both users and nearby peers." *Computers and Education 62*: 24-31.
ac.els-cdn.com/S0360131512002254/1-s2.0-S0360131512002254-main.pdf?_tid=823ea3 74-e0d7-11e5-bc6c-00000aab0f01&acdnat=1456965371ec0cd4c6b6bd860f0af9a30cdb 550e88

Smith, S. M., et al. (1978). "Environmental context and human memory." *Memory & Cognition 6(4)*: 342-353.
bjorklab.psych.ucla.edu/pubs/Smith_Glenberg_Bjork_1978.pdf

Verleger, R., et al. (2013). "Insights into sleep's role for insight: Studies with the number reduction task." *Advances in Cognitive Psychology 9(4)*: 160-172.
www.ncbi.nlm.nih.gov/pmc/articles/PMC3902672/pdf/acp-09-160.pdf

Further reading

Business
- Rework - Jason Fried and David Heinemeier Hansson

Cognitive Science
- How the Minds Works - Steven Pinker
- Incognito - David Eagleman
- The Organized Mind - Daniel Levitin
- The Scientist in the Crib - Alison Gopnik
- Thinking, Fast and Slow - Daniel Kahneman

Education
- Born to Rise - Deborah Kenny
- DIY U - Anya Kamenetz
- Free Range Learning - Laura Weldon
- Stop Stealing Dreams - Seth Godin
- The Test - Anya Kamenetz

Expertise
- The Art of Learning - Josh Waitzkin
- The Talent Code - Daniel Coyle

General Learning
- A Curious Mind - Brian Grazer
- Mastery - Robert Greene
- The Four-Hour Chef - Tim Ferriss

Intelligence
- 7 Kinds of Smart - Thomas Armstrong
- On Intelligence - Jeff Hawkins
- Smarter - Dan Hurley

Languages
- Fluent in 3 Months - Benny Lewis
- The Language Instinct - Steven Pinker

Math and Science
- How Not to Be Wrong - Jordan Ellenberg

Memory
- In Search of Memory - Eric Kandel
- Memory: From Mind to Molecules - Larry Squire & Eric Kandel
- Moonwalking with Einstein - Joshua Foer
- The Mind of a Mnemonist - Aleksandr Luria
- The Neurobiology of Learning and Memory - Jerry W. Rudy
- The Seven Sins of Memory - Daniel Schacter
- Total Recall - Gordon C. Bell

Neuroscience
- Choke - Sian Beilock
- Flow: The Psychology of Optimal Experience - Mihaly Csikszentmihalyi
- The Brain that Changes Itself - Norman Doidge

Psychology
- Being Wrong - Kathryn Schulz
- Mindset: The New Psychology of Success - Carol Dweck
- The Dip - Seth Godin
- The Power of Habit - Charles Duhigg
- Willpower - Roy Baumeister

Technology
- Smarter Than You Think - Clive Thompson

- Too Big to Know - David Weinberger

Writing

- Eats, Shoots & Leaves - Lynne Truss
- On Writing - William Zinsser
- The Sense of Style - Steven Pinker

Online resources

12 Rules for Learning Foreign Languages (Timothy Ferriss):
www.fourhourworkweek.com/2014/03/21/how-to-learn-a-foreign-language-2

2U — online degree programs from top-tier universities: www.2u.com

Academic Earth — free online courses from the world's top universities:
www.academicearth.org

AcaWiki — summaries of academic papers: acawiki.org

After the Deadline — checks for spelling and grammatical errors and provides style suggestions: www.polishmywriting.com

Audible — audiobooks and podcasts: www.audible.com

Blinkist — executive summaries of recent psychology, economics, finance, business, and classic books: www.blinkist.com

Carnegie Mellon University, Open Learning Initiative — online courses for anyone who wants to learn or teachk: oli.cmu.edu

Class Central — make informed online learning decisions: www.class-central.com

Coursera — free and paid courses from the top universities: www.coursera.org

Creative Commons — keeping the internet creative, free and open: www.creativecommons.org

Curious.com — play the game of lifelong learning: www.curious.com

Directory of Open Access Journals — online directory for high-quality, open access, peer-reviewed journals: www.doaj.org

Duolingo — learn Spanish, French, and other languages for free: www.duolingo.com

edX — free online courses from the world's best universities: www.edx.org

GoodReads — book reviews, recommendations, and discussion: www.goodreads.com

Google Books: www.books.google.com

Google Scholar: www.scholar.google.com

Internet Archive — library of millions of free books, movies, software, and more:
www.archive.org

italki — find native speakers and teachers online: www.italki.com

iTunes U (Open University): www.open.edu/itunes

Khan Academy — learn math, science, computer programming, history, art, economics, and more for free, includes interactive exercises with progress reports: www.khanacademy.org

Language Immersion for Chrome — translate everything in your browser to a desired language (easy, medium and hard modes): www.useallfive.com/work/language-immersion

Library Genesis — a Russian website where you can find free PDFs of books and textbooks: www.gen.lib.rus.ec

Lingua.ly — makes daily Internet use a language learning experience: www.lingua.ly

MIT OpenCourseWare — my personal favorite for teaching myself a new subject: ocw.mit.edu

NovoEd: www.novoed.com

OpenLearn: openlearn.open.ac.uk

Openstax CNX — view and share free educational material in small modules: www.cnx.org

Open Yale Courses: oyc.yale.edu

Quora — get the best answer to any question: www.quora.com

Similarsites.com — find sites similar to the ones you like: www.similarsites.com

Stanford Online: www.online.stanford.edu

Tai Lopez — How To Live the Good Life: www.tailopez.com

TED (Technology, Entertainment, Design) — short, powerful talks on new and important ideas: www.ted.com

The 4-Hour Workweek (Timothy Ferriss): www.fourhourworkweek.com '

Treehouse — computer programming: www.teamtreehouse.com

Udacity: www.udacity.com

Udemy — online courses anytime, anywhere: www.udemy.com

Unclasses: www.unclasses.org

What Should I Read Next — enter a book you like and receive a recommendation: www.whatshouldireadnext.com

Wikipedia: www.wikipedia.org

Wikiversity: en.wikiversity.org

Wolframalpha — incredibly powerful symbolic calculator, gives you access to the world's facts and data and calculates answers across a range of topics: www.wolframalpha.com

YouTube EDU: www.youtube.com/edu

How to help this book: a request

Thank you for reading my book! I hope it inspires you to rethink how you approach learning. If it somehow exceeded your expectations or left you feeling like, gee, the world would be better off if more people read this, then read further.

As you know by now, I'm a young, independent author. I don't have a multi-million dollar marketing machine behind me, the blessing of Penguin Random House, or a posse of billionaire friends. As a self-publisher, I am fully responsible for creating and promoting my book, and this is my first one. But if you're willing to chip in a few minutes of your time, you can seriously help this book find its way in this tough, cold market, where many helpful books never reach the people they should.

As none of the writing is worth the effort if the ideas aren't shared, please consider doing any of the following:
- Write a review on Amazon.com.
- Post about this book on your blog, on Facebook, on Twitter, or, even better, pose with the book and post a picture to Instagram.
- Recommend this book to your friends and your friends' friends and your mom's friends' kids and anyone else you think it might help.
- If you know people who write for magazines or newspapers or any other form of media, drop them a line.

Every little thing makes a difference. As an author, my opinion of the book carries surprisingly little weight. But you, dear reader, have all the influence in the world.

If you'd like to tweet or Instagram, the hashtag is #beyondbrilliance. If you have any questions for me or just want to say hi, feel free to email me at lucas@beyondbrilliance.org.

Acknowledgements

Very special thanks to Sahar Yousef—neuroscience PhD at Cal—who took me under her wing and showed me how deep this whole train-your-brain rabbit hole goes. This book wouldn't exist without her. To the team—Lauren Ouye (covers and illustrations), Akbar Khan (marketing and promotion), Jack Connolly (mobile application development), Lindsay Lewis (internal design), and Katrina Henry (editing)—thank you for your invaluable work and enthusiasm at all stages of this journey. I will be indebted to you for years to come.

For giving various honest feedback and providing generous positive support for my work (listed in a secret order I will never reveal): Katherine Redoglia, Bryce King, Gianna Spangler, Patricia Flynn, Ryan Chapman, Victoria Brown, Nathan Holmes, Sahand Saberi, Sohrob Nayebaziz, Sam Blaustein, Aneesh Prasad, Patrick Ong.

I also want to thank my family, my Kappa Alpha fraternity brothers at Berkeley, and other friends and supporters along the way, who kept me going when I thought I was too young, too inexperienced, or otherwise thought I wouldn't be able to deliver a valuable product.

To my financial backers, your faith in me formed the backbone of this whole project. From the bottom of my heart, thank you!

$50 and up:
Toren Berry, Travis Brashears, Daniel Hamilton, Nate Holmes, Kunal Marwaha, Andrew Miller, Parthiv Patel, Aneesh Prasad, Milad Razavi, David De Santis, Jawaad Tariq, Keith and Linda Bloom

$100 and up:
Chris Berry, Matt Casey, Ryan Chapman, Jackson Engles, Braxton Greco, Michael Hanlon, Grant Keene, Nishant Patel and Neha Sampat, Ian St. Louis

$250 and up:
David Shaw, Richard Miller, Zachary Miller, Carol Stroup, Eric and Ann Smyth

To the teachers and professors who changed my life and inexplicably set a time bomb for making me want to teach: Thomas Gerlach (Santa Margarita Catholic High School), Kate Graham (Santa Margarita Catholic High School), Lisa Taylor (Santa Margarita Catholic High School), Denis Auroux (UC Berkeley), Matthew Walker (UC Berkeley), and Ken Singer (UC Berkeley).

And here's a list of mostly people I don't know (some dead) who have inspired me in one way or another:

Seth Godin
Timothy Ferriss
Jason Fried
David Heinemeier Hansson
James Altucher
Sal Khan
David Eagleman
Gary Vaynerchuk
Ramit Sethi
Maria Popova
Robert Greene
Ray Dalio
Tai Lopez

Paul Minors
Venkatesh Rao
Deborah Kenny
Joshua Foer
Daniel Kahneman
Viktor Frankl
Sam Walton
Ricardo Semler
Sir Ken Robinson
Nelson Mandela
Benjamin Franklin
Dharmesh Shah
Warren Buffett

Made in the USA
Middletown, DE
04 April 2020